£1.20

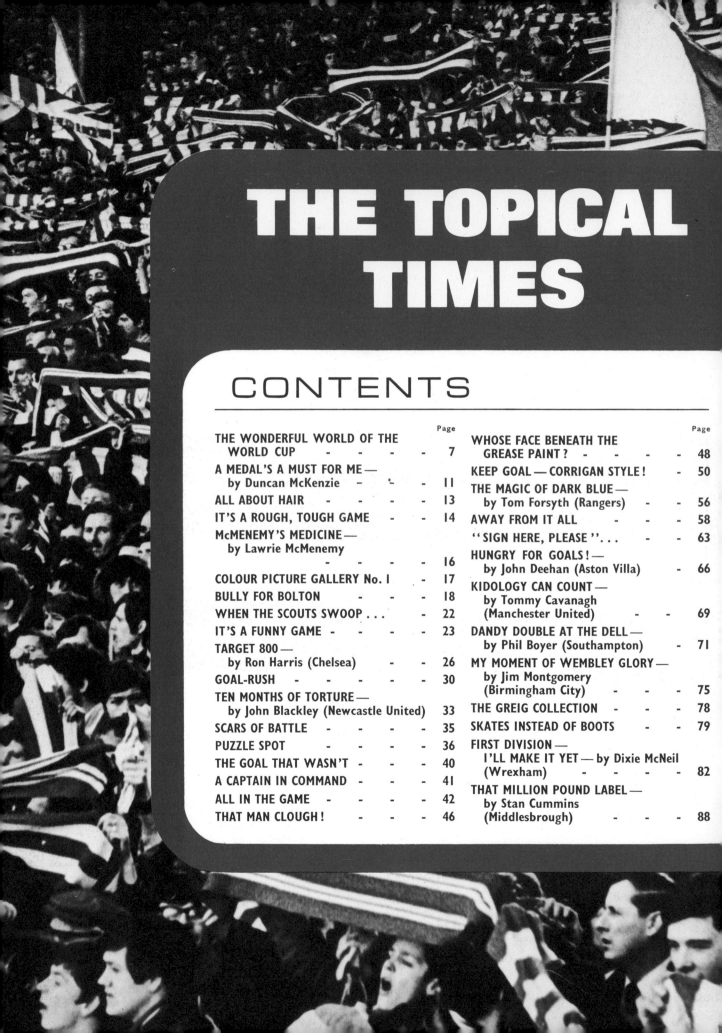

THE TOPICAL TIMES

CONTENTS

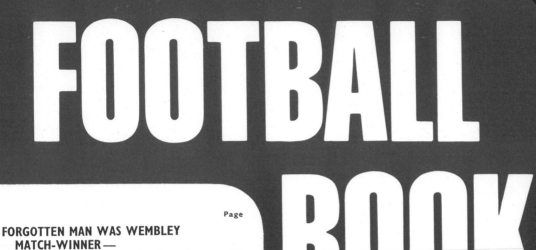

FOOTBALL BOOK 1979

● *All first-person articles as told to "Topical Times Football Book" writers.*

D. C. Thomson & Co., Ltd.
London – Manchester
Glasgow – Dundee

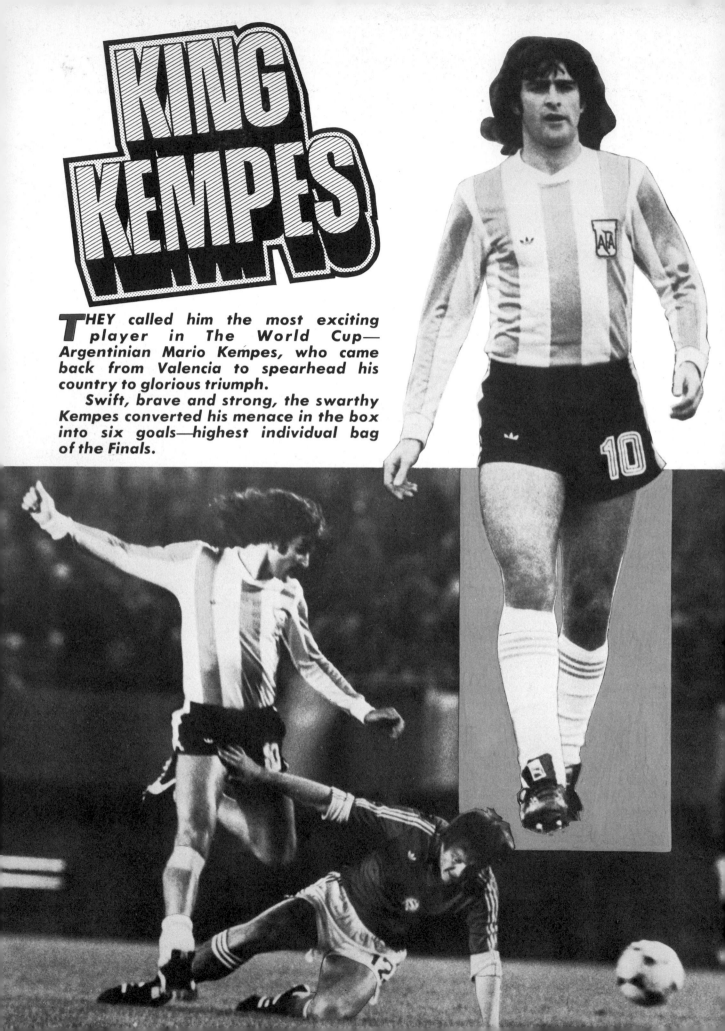

KING KEMPES

THEY called him the most exciting player in The World Cup—Argentinian Mario Kempes, who came back from Valencia to spearhead his country to glorious triumph.

Swift, brave and strong, the swarthy Kempes converted his menace in the box into six goals—highest individual bag of the Finals.

THE WONDERFUL WORLD OF

The WORLD CUP

WHEN Italian referee Sergio Gonella sounded the final whistle at the end of 120 torrid minutes in the last World Cup final at the spectacular River Plate Stadium in Buenos Aires, it was the signal for all Argentina to go mad.

From out of the night sky poured confetti. A confetti such as you have never seen before. Ticker tapes, invoices, and receipt slips. Shredded newspapers, letters and handbills. Old cheque stubs, telephone directories, and diaries.

Anything and everything that could be confettied and thrown into this national celebration came out of those skyscraper surroundings in Buenos Aires.

All accompanied by a thunderous blast, a bedlam made up of bongo drums, trumpets, bugles, car horns, klaxons,

(Continued on next page)

| MAGICAL SCOREBOARDS | FANTASTIC SUPERSTITIONS | INCREDIBLE STADIUMS |

WHERE LANGUAGE IS NO BARRRIER

hooters and the endless all-night chant of " AR-GEN-TINA, AR-GEN-TINA " from the thousands upon thousands who thronged the streets and squares.

For days after the final, the trees in the centre of Buenos Aires and in the vast 16-lane Avenida 9 de Julio were festooned with paper " leaves "—left-over from the confetti storm of that Sunday night of celebration.

A sight that was also to be seen in Cordoba, Mendoza, Rosario, Mar del Plata, and every other Argentine city and town and village.

For this was a nation en fete. A people having the chance to celebrate together. Having the chance to show a pride in their country such as they had not had in many a year.

A country bonded together by the performance of their football team. A team which,in earlier matches, had shown themselves the best in the tournament. But who, perhaps understandably, had let the standard of field behaviour drop in the final when they played with a " We must not lose " fervour that brought to mind a famous Bill Shankly-ism.

" Some people think football is a matter of life and death," said Bill. " In fact, it is a lot more serious than that."

Yet, whatever may be levelled against Argentine tactics in the final, there can be no denying they organised and ran a splendid World Cup final tournament.

Of course, they have F.I.F.A. to thank in large measure for that—as Spain are finding out at this moment.

For the Spanish hosts of World Cup '82 are already being pushed in the right direction under the firmest of guidance from the men who long ago blue-printed the ideal World Cup—the specialists who operate from F.I.F.A. headquarters in Zurich.

Let me take you behind the scenes for just one moment in any World Cup city you care to mention.

Imagine you have just been accepted as an accredited correspondent. You will have been given an identity tag with your picture on it and this you must display clipped to lapel or pocket if you wish entry to the luxurious Press Centre where you will do your work.

Every language is catered for. You are looked after like you were the most important person present. There is nothing but courtesy and helpfulness on all sides.

Yet they are careful, too. For everyone who comes in with a bag has it searched first.

On the ground floor there is a long counter staffed by girl interpreters. Before each is a notice giving the language she deals in. " English ", " French ", " German ", " Italian ", and so on.

And so to the Pressroom with its banks of portable typewriters—around 200 of them—with little desks and chairs and holders for copy paper.

Here, there is a continuing stream of news items and bulletins translated into ALL the languages.

Elsewhere on the other floors, there are Telex points (open 24 hours a day and sending to any part of the world via a bounce off a satellite), international telephone departments, photo-wiring facilities, a bank, a post office, bars, snack-bars and two restaurants.

All this duplicated at every one of the fantastically modern stadia that successive World Cups seem to demand.

An hour or so before the kick-off at any of these grounds, the Pressroom is a babel of sound. Spanish, German, Italian, English, French, Portuguese, Serbo-Croat, Arabic, Japanese. Think of a language and someone is speaking it.

In now, comes a very important V.I.P. indeed. A man as informal as he is important. The President of F.I.F.A. himself, Dr Joao Havelange, of Brazil.

He immediately gives you his hand. " You are from England or Scotland? Ah." And right away he slips into English for your benefit.

Up comes a newspaperman from France. Instant French it is from Havelange.

An Italian next. A Spaniard. No problem. Havelange has a word for all in their own tongue . . . and always finds time to give them time.

This one-time lawyer has presided over successive World Cups with the surest of touches and the discretion of a diplomat.

The man who announced on Cup Final eve itself that F.I.F.A. would have no objection if the fans in the River Plate Stadium threw—PAPER!

" You'll agree it is so much better than throwing bottles or stones," said Dr Havelange. " And there is no F.I.F.A. regulation which forbids the throwing of paper."

The F.I.F.A. President, of course, is only one of the many who throng the approaches to the World Cup stage and who seem ready to drop into almost any language of your choosing.

Women among men. At some F.I.F.A. Press Conferences all the simultaneous translators were women.

Seated in their glass boxes, earphones and microphones at the ready, they give completely calm and clear immediate translations of all that is going on at the conference. And all the reporter has to do is plug in his earpiece to the appropriate language.

Of course not all translators and interpreters are as spot-on in accuracy as those attached to F.I.F.A. headquarters. Fractured English is not hard to come by.

A speaker at one particular F.I.F.A. gathering in Moscow pulled out the old saying—" The spirit is willing but the flesh is weak."

Later he found to his horror that this had been translated for his Russian hosts as, " The vodka is good, but the meat is bad."

Then, during the Argentine finals, in Mendoza for the Scotland-Holland game, we came across a beauty in the official hand-out blurb about the magnificent new stadium.

There is probably no more spectacular ground than this anywhere in the world.

For a start, the pitch is below ground level. Indeed the whole stadium is constructed in one vast hole in the ground. Spectators enter by the turnstiles then walk DOWN the stairs to their places in stands or terracings.

They scored Holland's goals in qualification for the World Cup Final against Argentina — left, AREND HAAN and ERNY BRANDTS.

"BLACK PANTS BRING BAD LUCK"

SEPP MAIER, wearing his mighty gloves, is about to make a mighty throw.

THE MAN WITH THE OUTSIZE IN GLOVES

Sepp Maier, the West German goalkeeper, caused a lot of talk in Argentina by wearing enormous gloves. Specially designed, they were away ahead in size of those worn by other 'keepers — and some of their "mitts" were really massive.

The municipal authorities of Mendoza are proud about the entire ground being built and fitted out inside two years.

Yet, what happens but their brochure on the project proclaims—" First of all, two lawyers were laid beneath the turf."

Next sentence we were told—" Four other lawyers were laid from time to time and these were made up of stones and ashes and sand."

Amazing the difference a ' W ' can make in a word like " layer " . . .

Announcements in the World Cup Pressrooms, too, can often raise an eyebrow—or a smile.

As, for instance, the young lady who announced over the Buenos Aires Press Centre loudspeaker in impeccable accents—" We inform you that Saturday will not be carried out."

That, nothing more. We were left to wonder.

On, now, to match days themselves. Not all necessarily thrill-a-minute ties, but all with a very special atmosphere.

Take Scotland's opening tie—against Peru in Cordoba.

This was the very first World Cup game to be played in the brand new stadium, built some miles outside the city.

For the Cordobeses, it was the inauguration of the ground. A gala occasion. A huge, outdoor party. Almost anything, in fact, but a football match.

Before the start—and after the final whistle—dancers in full Latin-American rig slowly circled the entire pitch, dancing their way without a break to the fcct-tapping rhythms of a full orchestra set up on the wide stretch of green turf between grand-stand and track.

In the stand it was like being in the foyer of a theatre or concert hall before a big performance. There was much hand-shaking and cheek-kissing as families and friends met.

All very pleasant. All very civilised. But how different from the ear-splitting clamour which accompanied the Argentine and Brazilian teams wherever they were in action.

Wherever Argentine or Brazil were playing, the air was electric. Why, even the electronic scoreboards seemed to react more slickly when the two South American cracks were in action.

And weren't those Stewart-Warner boards just magic? I'm afraid they spoilt me for Britain's half-time boards for all time. They were a show in themselves as they performed all sorts of tricks.

Watching the word, " Gol," shoot up from one-line to full-screen size. Or the swift representation of goalmouth action. Or the trick of having one word chase another across the screen. Or the flipping on of a map of the world or of Argentina.

Anything seemed possible.

But of all the odd facts that go to make up the wonderful world of the World Cup, none, surely, is stranger or more unusual than the superstitions that abound.

Even the great Dutch team, finalists in the last two championships, confess they hate to wear black pants. Because, they say, it brings them bad luck.

" I honestly don't think we have ever won when we have had to wear them," says Johnny Rep.

In the Polish camp in Argentina there was a one-man personal " strike " when it became known Henry Kasperczak had been allocated the No 13 jersey.

It was unfair he should be loaded with the extra burden of a bad luck number, Henryk argued. There should be a ballot to see who should shoulder it.

What's more, the Polish manager, Jacek Gmoch, agreed. He promptly put all his squad's names into a waste-paper basket and drew out—Janusz Kupcewicz. And the happy Kasperczak immediately switched to No 8.

The Iran squad made a regular practice of kissing the Koran before taking the field. Indeed they preceded this by going out and kissing the turf immediately on arrival at a ground.

But most superstitious of all the squads in Argentina were the Peruvians.

Every man in the side wore amulets. Some two or three strung round their necks.

Weird and mysterious are the many individual ways of preparing for battle . . . even in the world's top tourney.

10   **STEVE WILLIAMS**, Southampton

A MEDAL'S A MUST FOR ME!

SAYS EVERTON'S EXCITING RAIDER
DUNCAN McKENZIE

THREE times I've been transferred for a fee of over £200,000. But it wasn't so long ago I was almost on my way to Third Division Mansfield on a " free ".

That was in my early days with Nottingham Forest. I was 19, out of the team and willing to settle for the lower leagues to get away.

Since then, of course, I've played for two of the greatest clubs in England—Leeds United and now Everton—plus a time with one of the top sides in Europe, Anderlecht of Belgium.

But I was very close to landing with Mansfield. I spent two separate spells there on loan from Forest.

Each time Forest decided to keep me. The second time was when Dave Mackay had arrived to take over the City Ground manager's chair. I found myself in the first team instead of in the reserves.

Dave gave me a free rein. The kind of job I'd done on my loan spells at Mansfield. It suited me.

In my first full season in the senior side I scored 28 times. Then, with Dave Mackay on his way to Derby, I was snapped up by Brian Clough, who had just taken over at Leeds.

Cloughie lasted only 44 days at Leeds. I stayed two seasons. Ending the second as top scorer with 16 goals.

But there were always four players for three forward places at Elland Road. Myself, Allan Clarke, Joe Jordan and Peter Lorimer. So it was difficult to hold down a regular first-team spot.

When the chance came to move to the Continent, I jumped at it.

Anderlecht offered me regular first-team football and a high standard of living.

I really enjoyed myself in Belgium. I played with and against the best players in Europe.

"HERE WAS THE CHALLENGE!"

Dutch World Cup stars, Rob Rensenbrink, and Arie Haan were in the same forward line. Because fewer league games were played there, we often turned out in friendlies against top continental sides.

Ajax, Borussia Moenchengladbach and St Etienne were among the teams we faced. That made up for the league standard being lower than in this country.

I would have loved to have stayed in Belgium. But, for family reasons, I decided to move back to Britain.

When I did, I found the ideal club in Everton.

They are rich, ambitious and play attractive

reckoned to be about 140 yards.

Getting back to the dressing-room I had another surprise. I was marched out into the car park to find the lads had set up the assistant secretary's Mini for me to jump.

I obliged with my party trick but things got a bit more serious when I agreed to repeat the feat before Paul Reaney's testimonial game.

There's a big difference doing something like that in front of a few mates and performing before a 20,000 crowd!

Flying high at Paul Reaney's testimonial match —

DUNCAN McKENZIE

football. They could be the team which will give me my first big honours in the game.

Strangely, I've never been in a trophy-winning side. Other than when Anderlecht lifted the European Super Cup.

I'm desperate for some kind of medal. The one I want most is the First Division Championship.

Aside from what I do on the field I guess I'm almost as well-known for activities off the park.

For instance I used to go around jumping over Minis. I've stopped this nowadays, though I often get requests to do the stunt for charity.

It began at Forest when I used to hurdle a five-bar gate to be first at the cold lemon drinks after training!

Then someone bet I couldn't leap a Mini. A car was rolled out at the City Ground and I cleared it.

I could also throw a golf ball considerable distances. But I thought both activities had been forgotten with my move to Leeds.

Suddenly, after a morning's training Norman Hunter produced a golf ball and said, " Let's see you do it then."

John O'Hare had told the Leeds lads about what I could do and here was the challenge.

So I took the ball out on to the pitch and flung it clean over the stand on the far side! The distance was

I had a touch of butterflies before the jump but I just managed it.

I still chuck a golf or cricket ball for a worthy cause, but that's about my lot these days.

Much of my time away from the club centres around my local radio programme. I team up on this with Liverpool and England goalkeeper Ray Clemence.

I used to have John Toshack as a partner but since Big Tosh took over as boss of Swansea, Ray has come in to provide the Liverpool half of the duo.

It's a sports programme with comment, chat and news on all sports. We also do interviews with various interesting personalities.

The programme goes out on a Sunday afternoon. The big talking point for Liverpool and Everton fans is our games the day before.

It's fun. It's lively. A great opportunity to explain our views to the fans. That's very important.

Fans have always been great to me. With every club I've been at I've struck up a good relationship.

I believe football is about entertaining the fans. Throughout my career that has been my aim.

Now I just hope I can add some kind of trophy to the entertainment. That is the major ambition I've my sights set on.

ALL ABOUT HAIR

Over the years football has seen many changes—and here's a line-up which shows how hairstyles have changed, too.

CHIC McINTOSH
LUTON TOWN
1930's

MATT BUSBY
MAN. CITY
1930's

TOMMY DOCHERTY
CHELSEA
1961

DEREK DOUGAN
WOLVES
1968

ALAN ROUGH
PARTICK THISTLE
1978

13

IT'S A ROUGH TOUGH GAME...

1. PETER CORMACK, Bristol City, is the meat in th[e] West Ham sandwich.
2. STEVE WICKS, Chelsea's No 6, takes it on the chi[n]

4. All in a tangle are FRANK STAPLETON, Arsenal (left) and KENNY BURNS, Forest.
5. BARRY KITCHENER, Millwall, shows the effort needed to beat Southampton's PHIL BOYER to a high ball.
6. Blood-stained DAVID GEDDIS, Ipswich, after scoring a winning goal against Arsenal.

2

3

3. STAN BOWLES, Q.P.R., is the man taking a nose dive.

6

7

7. The screwed-up faces tell the tale of the tough tackle between JOHN DEEHAN, Aston Villa, (left) and IAN GILLARD, Q.P.R.

McMENEMY'S MEDICINE

LAWRIE McMENEMY, who led Southampton to Division I last season, was star member of the Argentina World Cup TV panels.

Down to earth in criticism, realistic in praise, full of understanding about World Cup pressures, sympathetic to the luckless — he also showed great knowledge of foreign football.

Now, this man, who was on the short list for the job of England team manager, is looking ahead to the 1982 World Cup Finals in Spain.

SPAIN should be ideal for British qualifiers. The players know the country. Most have been there on family holidays. Most will have played there.

It will be a kind of home from home. There we have none of the problems that go with playing in South America. Particularly as regards food.

British fans also know Spain. They will flock there in their thousands. That will be great for British teams.

Of course, I must talk about England, I have no doubts at all that they will be involved in the Final stages of World Cup 1982. I think they will be joined by at least one other " home " country.

FIFA are suggesting the number of qualifiers in future should be increased from 16 to 24.

If this happens there must be a place for England — just as countries like East Germany, Russia, Czechoslovakia and Yugoslavia should be there.

By LAWRIE McMENEMY

The Final stages of the World Cup must involve the best teams in the world. Increasing the number for the Final competition would make sure this happens.

England's future is bright, I've seen a lot of the England youngsters, particularly the Under-21 side. Because I've had Steve Williams and David Peach, two of my Southampton players, involved with them.

I would like to see adopted the suggestion I made when interviewed for the job of England team manager. I made the point to the interviewing committee that the England Under-21 side should get together at least every month.

The youngsters could leave their clubs after the game on Saturday night and meet at a spot like Bisham Abbey. They could stay until Monday. Train together. Get to know each other.

There might be objections—from both clubs and players. We should get over this. A successful England team is good for the game. Any player not prepared to give up a week-end once a month is not England material.

After international matches, and the preparation involved, our players go back to their clubs. Back to managers with different ideas. By regular get-togethers of youngsters the England pattern would be kept flowing.

I feel it would also change our approach to the game. Necessarily so. Teams like Tunisia and Iran showed us what emerging countries have learned.

Frank O'Farrell was on the BBC-TV panel with me. He had no doubts about the skills of Iran, whom he had coached, being of world class. His doubts were about their ability to be as strong as the top teams from Europe and South America.

Iran proved these doubts misplaced. Against Scotland they showed both skill and stamina.

So the newer countries will almost certainly make an even bigger impact on the 1982 World Cup than did Iran and Tunisia in Argentina.

The old and the new are getting closer over the years.

As far as we are concerned I feel we take the game just a little too much for granted. We feel that, as we have always played football, our young players know all about the game.

We must forget that and go back to the same standard of early teaching. Giving our young players the same basic skills—before we start talking about tactics and all the rest of it.

This is something I would like to do with young apprentice professionals. It has been traditional for the apprentices to clean the training boots of their "betters".

I worked it out that cleaning thirty pairs of boots takes something like an hour. I feel the youngsters would be better employed learning simple skills, starting with controlling and passing the ball. So the seniors could clean their own practice boots. Or a man called in to do the job.

Kevin Keegan is the best example of how hard we must work at our game. When he left Liverpool for Hamburg he seemed to be at his peak. An England man. An ace in Liverpool's first European Cup success.

Since he's been with Hamburg, Kevin thinks (and I think) he is an even better player. Every game he has played for England confirms this point.

During the Argentina World Cup I talked to Kevin, who was on the other TV panel. He told me Hamburg players get a three-week break at the end of the season and that he had been given an extra three days leave to talk about the World Cup.

In Britain we have a close season that covers at least a couple of months.

Kevin Keegan is working longer and harder at the game—and benefiting. We must do the same in the years between now and the big show in Spain.

And I can't think of a better place to start putting Britain back on the World Cup map.

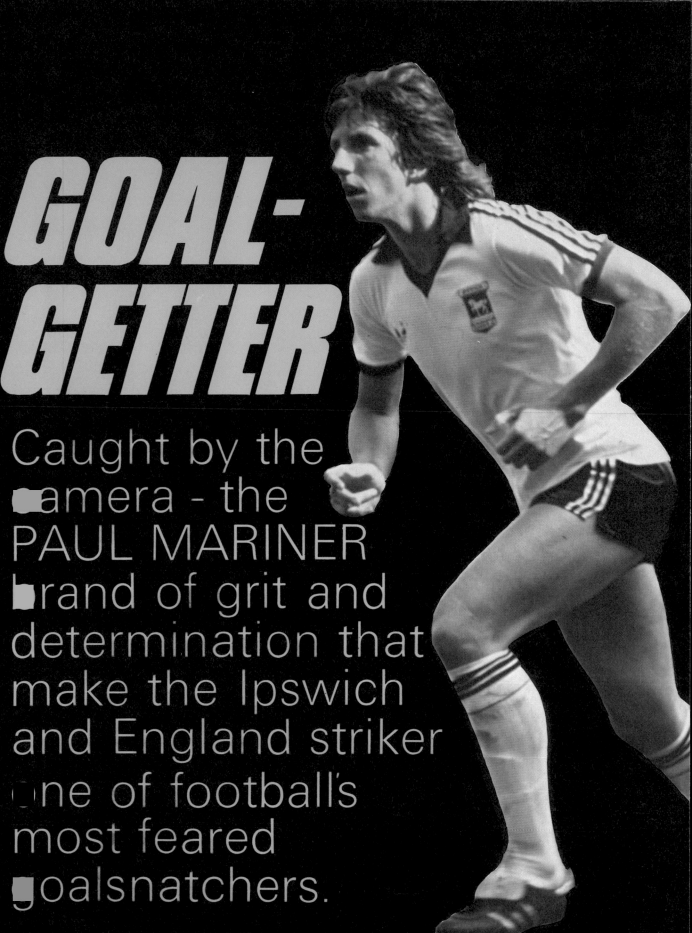

GOAL-GETTER

Caught by the camera - the PAUL MARINER brand of grit and determination that make the Ipswich and England striker one of football's most feared goalsnatchers.

Bolton boss, IAN GREAVES — he finished the job

A FAMOUS name in football, Bolton Wanderers have a history packed with great names and exciting matches but none more memorable than their appearance in the first-ever Cup Final at Wembley in 1923.

Today in the panelled board-room at Burnden Park, Wanderers display a huge photograph of the amazing scenes from that 1923 Cup Final — known as " The White Horse Final."

Bolton's opponents were West Ham United. Wembley, newly opened, was described as the " largest, most comfortable and best equipped stadium in the world, holding more than 125,000 people."

An hour before kick-off, the police realised there was going to be a massive attendance.

Inner gates and stairways were closed, except to ticket holders. But the pressure of the crowd burst some of the barriers and elsewhere supporters climbed over the railings.

By three o'clock the crowd was estimated at more than 150,000. The pitch was covered with milling fans.

But the now famous policeman on the white horse and his colleagues helped to clear the playing area. The crowd was pushed back to the touchlines, and the game started forty minutes late. Bolton ran out 2-1 winners.

Ever since that day, the F.A. Cup has held a special place in the Bolton club. But that was not the last time Bolton were to figure in a cup final.

In 1926 they were back at Wembley, defeating Manchester City 1-0. In 1929 they again won the Cup, beating Portsmouth 2-0.

Bolton also featured in one of the most exciting Cup Finals played — in 1953.

Wanderers' opponents were Blackpool, who had the famous Stanley Matthews in their team.

In the Bolton team was another famous England forward — Nat Lofthouse. Nicknamed the " Lion Of Vienna " after his courageous display in an England victory over Austria, he was Bolton's key man.

And it was Nat Lofthouse who gave Bolton the lead in only two minutes. Blackpool equalised but after ten minutes of the second half, Bolton seemed to have the cup won when Bell scored their third. But then Blackpool scored twice to equalise, setting the scene for a dramatic finish.

Time after time the ball was sent out to Matthews. And in the dying seconds the winger gave a perfect pass to Perry, who slammed home the winner.

But Wanderers were back at Wembley again in 1958. And this time they won the Cup, beating by 2-0 Manchester United, who had lost the nucleus of their team in the Munich air disaster.

It was a great day for the Wanderers. Not only had they beaten their local rivals, but they did so with a team made up completely of home-produced players — none cost more than the £10 signing-on fee.

BULLY FOR BOLTON

But Bolton's F.A. Cup story has not been all happy memories and Wembley appearances.

In 1946, 33 spectators died and 500 were injured when crush-barriers collapsed at Burnden Park before a sixth-round match against Stoke City.

Whilst the F.A. Cup has been in the Burnden Park trophy-room four times, the club have never won the First Division title, even though they were one of the original members of the Football League in 1888.

In the hills north of Bolton lies a village called Chapeltown, in the rural borough of Turton. Here, in 1871, Turton F.C. was formed. The club colours were described in their handbook as " blue knickerbockers, white stockings and white jerseys." These are Bolton Wanderers' colours to this day.

Turton F.C. was talked about all over Lancashire. And fired by their example, Thomas Ogden, a schoolmaster from Christ Church School, Bolton, decided to form his own team in 1874.

Ogden based his club on the Turton set-up. And three years later, it was decided to change their name from Christ Church to Bolton Wanderers.

To this day, football is still played on that small ground in Chapeltown, now owned by amateurs Old Boltonians.

That village field seems a million miles from Burnden Park 1978 style, with its social club, television and video-tape gantry, floodlights and massive terracing. Now back in the First Division, Bolton have emerged from the most difficult part of their history.

Relegated from the top flight in 1964, their decline continued right through the '60's until, in 1971, Bolton sank into the Third Division for the first time ever.

But then Jimmy Armfield arrived to take charge, and he led the club to the Third Division title in 1973.

When Armfield left to take over at Leeds, his deputy, Ian Greaves, completed the job.

One hundred and one years old, Bolton look set for a future as bright as their past.

PETER KITCHEN, Orient

19

WHAT THE WELL-DRESSED FOOTBALLER IS WEARING

A sharp-shooter on the field, Bolton Wanderers' Frank Worthington is a sharp dresser in his off-the-field gear.

PETER SHILTON, Nottingham Forest

MAURICE LINDLEY, now assistant manager of Leeds United, has pulled off many a signing scoop when a scout.

The one he'll never forget happened at the end of a hair-raising car journey to Scotland with his boss at the time, Don Revie.

It almost landed him in trouble with the police.

It DID land Peter Lorimer for Leeds United.

"We had long had a strong fancy for Peter Lorimer," says Maurice. "He was cracking tremendous shots into the net even as a kid in Dundee. This of course attracted a lot of attention from other clubs.

"Don Revie was tipped off we might lose out as Manchester United were due to speak to Lorimer next day.

"I got a 'phone call from Don and off we went by car. Dundee is around 260 miles

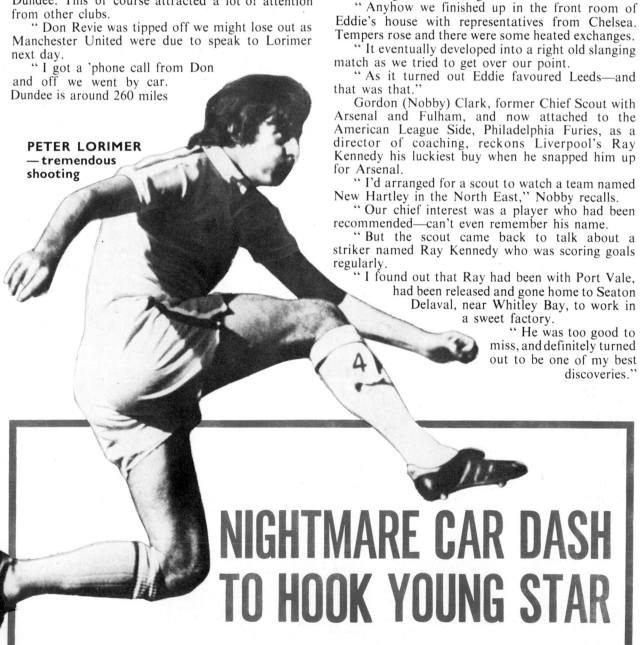

PETER LORIMER — tremendous shooting

from Leeds, but we were there in about four hours.

"We were stopped by the police in Perth for speeding. Don explained who he was and what was his mission and they let us off.

"I've never had such a hairy drive in my life. But thinking of what Lorimer has done for Leeds, it was worth every bump."

As a schoolboy Eddie Gray was reckoned the hottest prospect in years. The chase for his signature was no less hectic than that for Lorimer's.

"A whole lot of clubs had made approaches", says Lindley. "In the end it was with ourselves or Chelsea. As we had been first to declare an interest we felt it gave us the edge."

"Anyhow we finished up in the front room of Eddie's house with representatives from Chelsea. Tempers rose and there were some heated exchanges.

"It eventually developed into a right old slanging match as we tried to get over our point.

"As it turned out Eddie favoured Leeds—and that was that."

Gordon (Nobby) Clark, former Chief Scout with Arsenal and Fulham, and now attached to the American League Side, Philadelphia Furies, as a director of coaching, reckons Liverpool's Ray Kennedy his luckiest buy when he snapped him up for Arsenal.

"I'd arranged for a scout to watch a team named New Hartley in the North East," Nobby recalls.

"Our chief interest was a player who had been recommended—can't even remember his name.

"But the scout came back to talk about a striker named Ray Kennedy who was scoring goals regularly.

"I found out that Ray had been with Port Vale, had been released and gone home to Seaton Delaval, near Whitley Bay, to work in a sweet factory.

"He was too good to miss, and definitely turned out to be one of my best discoveries."

NIGHTMARE CAR DASH TO HOOK YOUNG STAR

Nowhere is football rivalry keener than on Merseyside—and here are some of the big names that give Liverpool and Everton fans something to shout about.

BOB LATCHFORD
Everton

DAVID JONES
Everton

MIKE PEJIC
Everton

RIVALS

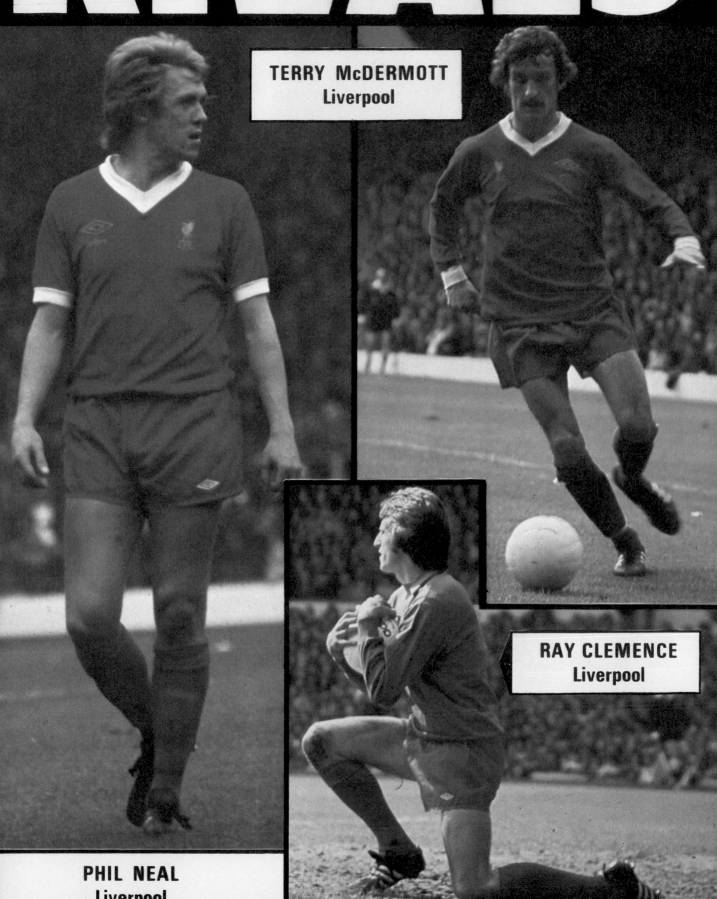

TERRY McDERMOTT
Liverpool

RAY CLEMENCE
Liverpool

PHIL NEAL
Liverpool

TARGET 800–

CHELSEA'S RON HARRIS TAKES AIM

SOME folk are inclined to think I'm almost as old as the Chelsea club itself.

Well, I joined as a junior in August, 1960, and signed professional in November, 1961. Eighteen years I'll never forget.

There's so much to remember.

Winning the European Cup-Winners Cup, the FA Cup and the League Cup. Being part of the side that put Chelsea back in the 1st Division—even if I spent the majority of games sitting on the touchline as substitute.

Helping re-establish Chelsea as a 1st Division side last season—and looking forward to the next couple of seasons.

I'd like to take a closer look at these eighteen years at Stamford Bridge.

First—the time I was skipper of the England side that won the " Little World Cup " at Wembley in 1963.

We topped a section that included Holland, Russia, and Rumania. We beat Scotland in the semi-final and Northern Ireland in the final .

So many players from these matches went on to become big soccer names—Pat Jennings (Arsenal), Jon Sammels (Leicester), George Graham (Crystal Palace), Peter Lorimer (Leeds) and Tommy Smith (Liverpool).

That wasn't my only experience of Wembley. I'd skippered an England schoolboy side there and was the then youngest FA Cup Final skipper when Chelsea lost to 'Spurs in 1967.

I was back on the winning side when we beat Leeds United in a 1970 Cup replay at Old Trafford. Another high point was the Cup Winners' Cup in Athens a year later, when Chelsea beat Real Madrid 2-1.

Great years for Chelsea. And I'm sure the present young side can prove as capable of winning top honours.

MY GREATEST PLAYER

I've skippered the England Under-23 side, but never won a " full " cap. Perhaps that is the one regret about my playing career.

In my time with Chelsea I've often been given an odd nickname—" Bomber " or " Chopper "

As far as games at Stamford Bridge are concerned you know that's a friendly " handle ". Away from home—perhaps it carries just a little more bite.

My job in football has always been to close mark and tackle. It makes you a " hero " at home—a "villain" when playing away. But the forwards you have to mark appreciate the position.

When I first arrived at Stamford Bridge, Jimmy Greaves was the big star. By the time I'd won a place in the Chelsea side, he was with 'Spurs.

I was always detailed to mark him.

Jimmy would say " What, you again!" and I'd stick to him like glue for the full ninety minutes.

I think I close-marked Jimmy Greaves in some eighteen matches—and he never scored a goal.

The greatest player I ever marked was Denis Law. He had everything. Good in the air, two good feet, quick and competitive. If he found himself close-marked around the penalty area, he'd drift off into mid-field and still have an influence on the game.

Of current players I'd say Kenny Dalglish is much the same. I had to mark Dalglish in an F.A. Cup tie at Stamford Bridge last season. I kept him reasonably quiet—but he was so much like Denis Law. You never knew what he was to do next.

We had a tremendous battle—and shook hands at the end. That's the way it usually is. Players always respect each other.

If I were asked the biggest change in the game I would say the treatment of the young players.

Big transfer fees have made it essential for clubs to develop their own young men.

As a youngster at Chelsea I collected £8 a week. For that I was expected to clean boots, sweep down the terraces and do all the odd chores around the ground.

Then I'd train in the afternoon—and feel on top of the world if I got a training session with the reserves. Over the moon if I played in a first team training game.

Now young players are rushed. A few games in the reserves and they have arrived. Half a dozen first team games and they are labelled stars.

Some players can take it. Others can't. The build-up nowadays is faster, but I think it did all us old-timers a lot of good to clean the boots.

Another big change in football is the approach to the game is much more defensive. A few seasons ago teams were inclined to go out to play off-the-cuff football. You were under orders to cut out the danger men, but generally you were left to your own devices.

Nowadays everything is so much tighter. Managers have to produce results, so there is a lot more playing to a set pattern. Not so much improvisation.

You mark " zones ", " areas ", " space ".

Freedom is perhaps the hall-mark of a " great " player. The ability to do the unexpected. Greaves, Law, Dalglish, Alan Ball, Peter Osgood, when he was with Chelsea, or our current skipper, Ray Wilkins—these are the names that come to mind.

RAY WILKINS — hallmark of greatness

I've had some wonderful times as a professional footballer. Including travelling on tours all over the world.

I've spent my entire career with a club I have never thought of leaving. Not even when I was sacked as skipper in 1972. Then we had a bad spell. After a fifth round FA cup defeat by Orient, we were beaten by Stoke City in the League Cup Final.

I was dropped because Dave Sexton, then Chelsea manager, felt that being skipper affected my form.

But I was soon back into the side—and have been in the first-team pool ever since.

I do still take over as captain on odd occasions, such as the FA Cup tie against Liverpool last season. Ray Wilkins (skipper) and Micky Droy (club captain) were out of the side and I got the job.

Football has been good to me. I'd like to put something back into the game. Perhaps in a coaching role. But that's a good way off. Say another couple of seasons.

I've played more than 700 games for Chelsea. Now I'd like to hit the 800 target. That would be something!

JOHN RICHARDS, Wolves

TWO IN A TANGLE
RONNIE GLAVIN, Celtic, (wearing
no. 4) tussles with ANDY ANDERSON,
Partick Thistle.

GLYN JONES

IT was a big day for 18-year-old Bristol Rovers' goalkeeper, Glyn Jones. His third first team game was at White Hart Lane against promotion-hunting Tottenham Hotspur. But, 90 minutes later, Glyn's big day had turned sour—Rovers had lost 9-0!

Nine days later, Glyn Jones was back at White Hart Lane—playing for Bristol Rovers' reserves against Spurs' reserves. After the game—which ended in a 1-1 draw—a Spurs' fan approached the young, keeper and asked if he wanted a programme that Spurs had had printed for the previous home game, showing each of the nine goals.

Glyn Jones took three programmes—and tucked them away as a constant reminder of that White Hart Lane goal rush.

1 Colin Lee slips home the first.

2 A powerful header by Lee notches the second.

3 A desperate dive by the goalkeeper can't stop Peter Taylor scoring the third.

4 Number four comes from Ian Moores.

5 Colin Lee hits his third and Spurs' fifth.

6 Glyn Jones beaten for the sixth time.

7 Ian Moores completes his hat-trick.

8 Colin Lee brings his tally to four.

9 Hoddle gets his name on the score sheet for number nine.

COLIN LEE

GOAL RUSH

ALBION ACE

— CYRILLE REGIS
West Bromwich Albion

EXPLOSIVE is the way to describe the impact Cyrille Regis has had on the football scene—and explosive is certainly the way to describe this raider's play.

Fast and fearless with a cracking shot in either foot—these are the qualities that have made Regis one of football's top strikers.

A bargain buy at £5,000 from non-league Hayes, Regis has established himself in the Albion team and earned a place in the England Under-21 squad—with that full cap looming on the horizon in the not too distant future.

On the club scene, his exciting play did much to give West Bromwich Albion their impressive cup run last season and help them win a place in Europe.

For Cyrille Regis—action is the name of the game!

TEN MONTHS OF TORTURE

THAT was a season that was! The craziest of my entire footballing career. It was all ups and downs. I felt a bit like a yo-yo at times.

Yet last term started just like any one of the previous 12 I had spent with Hibs in the Scottish League.

The only difference was that when it kicked off I had high hopes of going to Argentina with Scotland for the World Cup finals.

However, when World Cup time came around a lot had happened to me . . .

I'd joined Newcastle United. Suffered the worst run of injury in my career. Been relegated to the English Second Division. And then I failed to make the final 22 for the Argentine!

With the "downs" out-weighing the "ups", it would be easy to say I made the wrong decision when I said yes to my £100,000 transfer.

I can honestly admit, however, that even if I could turn the clock back to October '77 I would still do the same thing. I have absolutely no regrets.

The move to Newcastle was a dream come true for me. I was 29 at the time. And after more than a decade in Scottish football I felt the chance of playing in England had passed me by.

So it was a surprise when I discovered Newcastle wanted to sign me. Believe me, I jumped at the chance.

JOHN BLACKLEY
(Newcastle United)
looks back on his craziest-ever season

BACK IN THE TOP FLIGHT AGAIN

I had no hesitation in making the move. Despite the fact I knew Newcastle were already deep in relegation trouble.

I knew exactly what I was letting myself in for.

As it turned out "demotion" WAS Newcastle's lot at the end of the season. Despite half expecting it, I was still pretty choked about it all.

The fact I'm playing in the Second Division this season hasn't disheartened me. The soccer fans of Tyneside have seen to that!

I always felt I had a good relationship with Hibs' supporters during my days at Easter Road. But the way the Geordie folk accepted and took to me on my arrival is something else altogether. They're very special, believe me.

Within weeks they'd made me feel as if I'd spent my entire career at St James's Park. And the fact I was voted United's Player-of-the-Year was just the icing on the cake.

Don't forget, I joined the club at a time when the fans had little to cheer or enthuse about. It's even been said last season was the worst and most depressing in Newcastle's history.

Yet they showed amazing loyalty. Not only to me, but to other players as well. In my case it wasn't that they saw all that much of me. Certainly not as much as I would have liked.

With Hibs I can barely remember missing more than a couple of games on the trot through injury. But almost as soon as I set foot in St James's Park I was a regular on the treatment table.

The main problem was with my ankles. But, as so often happens, this also led to a succession of niggling little pulls and strains elsewhere.

I missed more games than I played as the team battled to stay in the First Division. Being so often unable to play my part was a real sickener.

I've no doubt either that the injury problems proved a factor in my failure to make the Scotland party for Argentina.

Similarly being a member of an unsuccessful side couldn't have done my chances any good, either.

But even if fully fit, I'd have needed to hit top form to pip Kenny Burns of Nottingham Forest.

I'm sure it was between the two of us for that place in the Argentina squad. The way Kenny played last season he deserved to go.

But, though missing out was obviously a terrible disappointment, there is no way I blame Newcastle. I accept it as all part of the game.

What is a little upsetting, however, is that the Argentine was probably my last chance of playing in the World Cup.

I'm now 30. It's hard to imagine I'll be considered again in another four years.

I would expect younger players will be filling the international jerseys by then. I'd be the last to argue against that. Football is all about progress.

The disappointment and upset of last season has got to be pushed to the background. The future is what counts most.

In Newcastle's case I would like to think the end of the season will see the club back in the top flight again. Not only that but battling at the very top of the pile for every honour in the game.

I'm still as ambitious as the day I set out in football. I believe Newcastle can satisfy some of that ambition.

Maybe that sounds a bit strange coming after a season in which we were relegated. But I honestly believe the potential of the club is unlimited. I wouldn't have joined them otherwise.

Above all else, however, I believe the people of Tyneside deserve the "very best" team in the land.

It's my aim to help give them just that!

KENNY BURNS
— he deserved his place

THE SCARS OF BATTLE

CUP-TIES are always hard-fought encounters—and the Ipswich v West Bromwich Albion semi-final in April 1978, was no match for the faint-hearted.

So, when Albion's JOHN WILE took an early head knock—there was no thought of leaving the pitch. He played on till half-time—then, heavily bandaged, he was back in the fray in the second-half. Ipswich won the game—but the courage of John Wile will always be remembered.

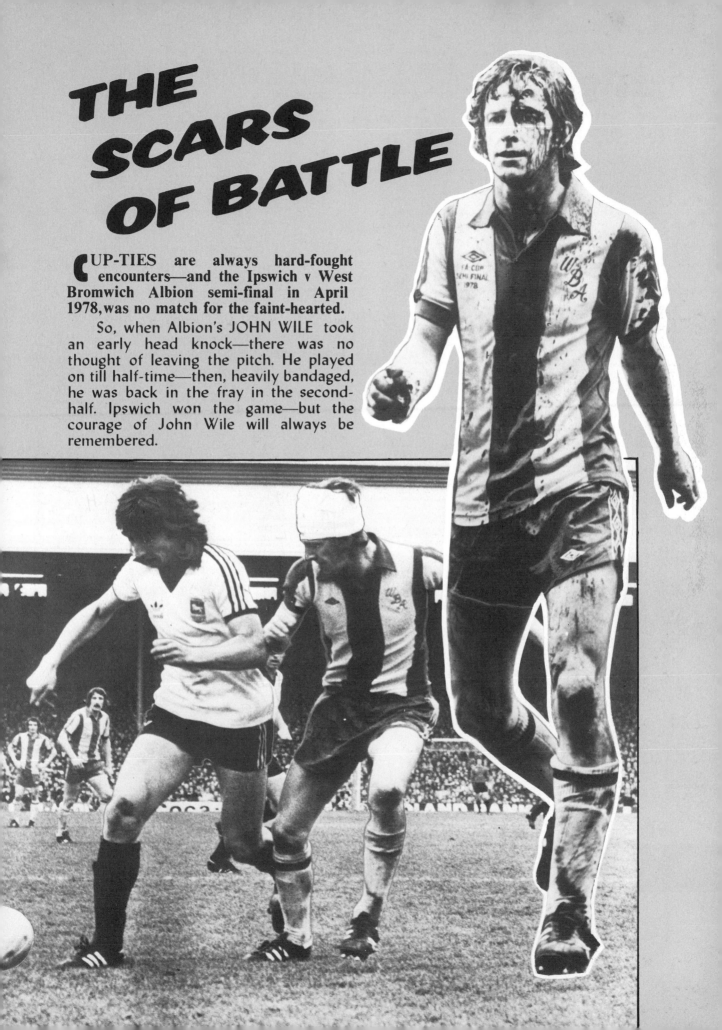

PUZZLE SPOT

FAMOUS FACE
Who is the famous player whose name consists of these letters?

LETTER LINKS.
Start top left-hand corner and then move down, across or diagonally to spot eight players.

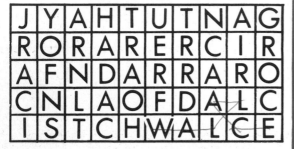

J	Y	A	H	T	U	T	N	A	G
R	O	R	A	R	E	R	C	I	R
A	F	N	D	A	R	R	A	R	O
C	N	L	A	O	F	D	A	L	C
I	S	T	C	H	W	A	L	C	E

Re-arrange the letters shown below and you'll spot the names of six football clubs—

1—AAAACCDEHIILLMMNOST   2—ABBCEHIILMNOORSTWW
3—ABDEELNNOORRSTW   4—AEFGHIMNNOORSTT
5—AAACDEEELNRRWX   6—ACDEEEFHIILLMNNRTTU

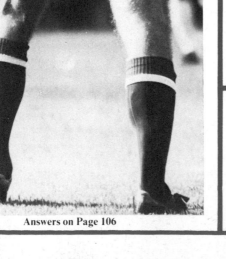

WHOSE LEGS ARE THESE?
A different view of a well-known London striker. Can you name him?

Answers on Page 106

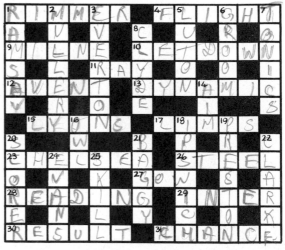

Complete this pyramid with Arsenal's aid. Here are the clues to the missing football personalities or clubs—

1—London player with famous cricket namesake (3).
2—Sir has layed, managed and directed (5).
3—A faithful servant at Stamford Bridge (7).
4—Brothers who have played together at Old Trafford (9).
5—They are known as The Cobblers (11).
6—Arthur Rowe, Bert Head and Malcolm Allison have managed them (7,6).

CROSSWORD

ACROSS. 1. Aston Villa and England goalkeeper (6). 4. A Continental trip perhaps (6). 9. Coventry manager (5). 10. Big disappointment (3—4). 11. Clemence to his pals (3). 12. Competition (5). 13. Forceful (7). 15. Everton player with a French connection (5). 17. Walks lamely (5). 23. London club (7). 26. One-time man of mettle for Scotland (5). 27. Bristol City Scot. 28. Studious team? (7) 29. Italian aces (5). 30. Rustle one up on a Saturday! (6). 31. Opportunity knocks! (6).

DOWN. 1. Former England manager (6). 2. Brighton boss (7). 3. Club led on by a tennis player? (7). 5. English Second Division side (5). 6. Prepare for stardom (5). 7. Pick-me-ups (6). 8. Scottish team down by the riverside (3). 14. Target (3). 16. Nickname for a Wednesday player (3). 18. Once managed by one down (7). 19. Team that kept going? (7). 20. Marksman (6). 21. Plants used in the Alec James era (5). 22. Allan of Leeds and England (6). 24. A Welsh-sounding player (5). 25. Craftsmanship (5).

How few of the following facts do you need before identifying a club?

1—They entered the English Second Division in 1908.
2—Their record victory is 13—2 v. Crewe Alexandra.
3—They won the European Cup Winners Cup in 1962-63.
4—They achieved the Football League—F.A. Cup double in 1960-61.
5—Their top scorer for one season and on aggregate is Jimmy Greaves.
6—They play at White Hart Lane.

36

IT'S A GOAL!

It was PAUL McGHEE'S first for Queen's Park Rangers—and he made no secret of his jubilation.

LIAM BRADY, Arsenal

JIM HOLTON, Coventry City

THE GOAL THAT WASN'T

NOTTINGHAM FOREST striker Peter Withe was jubilant when he found the net against Leeds United. But when the referee disallowed the goal, joy turned to dismay—as you can see!

CONGRATULATIONS FROM TONY WOODCOCK.

"IT'S A GOAL!"

A PAT ON THE BACK.

WHAT, NO GOAL?

BUT, REF . . .

A CAPTAIN IN COMMAND

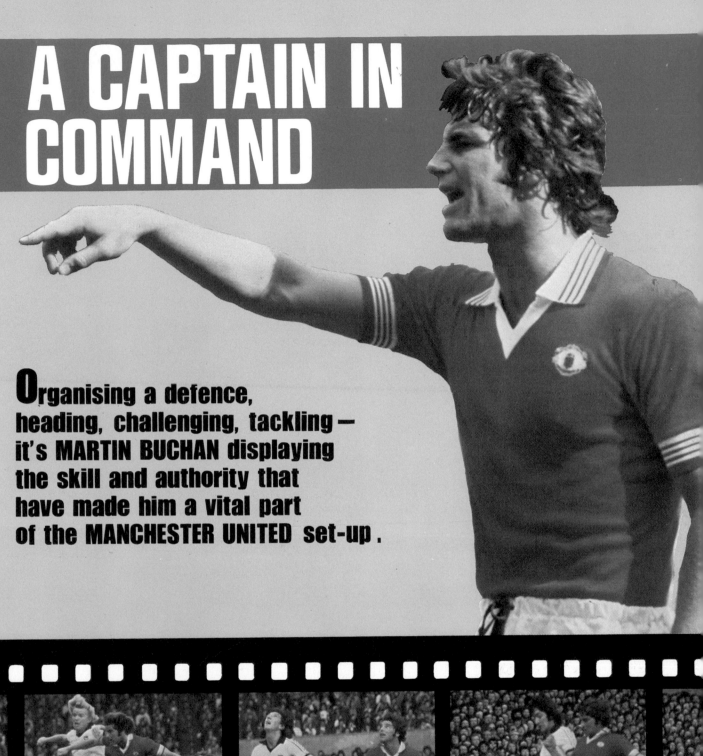

Organising a defence, heading, challenging, tackling — it's MARTIN BUCHAN displaying the skill and authority that have made him a vital part of the MANCHESTER UNITED set-up.

ALL IN THE GAME!

In an Irish minor league game, the referee decided to caution a player. The offender was so incensed at the referee's action that he tore up the ref's notebook!

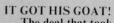

SHIRT TALE

After almost every international game, the players exchange jerseys— but in Uruguay the national players are paying for the privilege.

The Uruguayan FA, short on funds, can't afford to provide new shirts for each game.

So the rule in Uruguay now is ... swop your shirt and you have to pay for it.

When a group of Bristol City supporters bought a racehorse, they found just the right name for it— ROYLE HUNTER, a tribute to Bristol City players, Joe Royle and Norman Hunter.

MIXED-UP MANAGER

A West German manager was overjoyed when his team won a U.E.F.A. Cup-tie first leg 4—0. But joy turned to disappointment when they won the second leg as well ... Puzzled?

The reasoning is simple. Gyula Lorant the manager involved, had steered Eintracht Frankfurt to a comfortable win over Bayern Munich. However, before the second leg, Lorant had become Bayern's new boss!

IT GOT HIS GOAT!

The deal that took Italian mid-fielder Guiseppe Murgia from the amateur Sardinian team, Polisportira, to Seulese, must surely rate as one of the strangest ever. Murgia was bought for one goat and a slice of ham.

The transfer was seen as a protest against high transfer fees in Italy.

There has never been another goal in the Football League like one scored for Chelsea at Stamford Bridge, in December 1954.

Leicester City defenders, Stanley Milburn and Jack Froggatt, kicked the ball simultaneously into their own goal. "I couldn't separate them," said the referee.

Footballers aren't usually pleased when they're "on the carpet." But Ipswich's Brian Talbot (left) and Paul Mariner, were all smiles when they inspected their club's new training pitch which is made from nylon ribbon knitted to form a carpet.

When First Division Dundee played a home match against St Johnstone, they hit on this unusual way of greeting their fans.

During a game in the Wild West of the Argentinian pampas between Racing Cruz and Estoril Mendoza, one fan, annoyed at the ref's decisions, tried to teach him the ropes!

He ran on to the pitch and lassoed the official. It took the police ten minutes to free the roped-up ref.

When Peruvian Champions, Deportivo Huaral, went through a serious financial crisis, they couldn't afford to pay for new football boots. Manager Moises Barack had to name his side according to the sizes of boots he could find!

"KITCHEN SINKS NORWICH"
This headline caught the eye and set us looking for other footballers whose names made snappy headlines. Here's some that fit the bill.
LOCK KEEPS 'EM OUT
EVERYONE BEATEN BY BIRCH
CASE DISMISSED
GUNN ON TARGET
PIPER PLAYS ON
BUTCHER GETS THE CHOP
BALL BOUNCES BACK
SAVED BY SALVAGE
FORWARDS TAMED BY WYLDE
PENNY PAYS HIS WAY
PEACH PICKED
SCALES WEIGHS UP OPPOSITION

Policemen on duty at the Manchester United v St Etienne European Cup Winners' Cup game kept a sharp eye for trouble —whichever direction it came from!

44   **STEVE PERRYMAN**, Spurs

DAVID NISH, Derby County 45

FOR many, Nottingham Forest manager, Brian Clough is a man of mystery. A highly successful boss with Derby County and Forest, and yet a man with two very different images.

When he won the First Division title with Derby he was the tough talking T.V. critic. Always outspoken and the centre of a storm of argument.

With Forest with whom he has achieved an even bigger success, he is seldom heard—often refusing requests for interviews. Seen only in glimpses when the cameras catch him on the Forest bench.

But to those who know him, Brian Clough has not changed since he was banging in 40 goals a season as Middlesbrough's centre-forward in the early 1960's.

Even in those days he ruffled feathers with his burning desire to make his team the best in the business.

Middlesbrough were an easy-going club and that didn't suit the young Cloughie.

Often the team coach would not travel with them to away games.

On Monday mornings on the training field he would be told about any mistakes and would attempt to sort them out.

It was Brian Clough who marched up to the manager to tell him this was ridiculous. That the coach should be there to see for himself.

Clough wasn't popular but the club knew he was right and the coach travelled to every game from then on.

A knee injury cut short Clough's playing career at the age of 28, in 1964. It was the toughest blow he ever knew, having lived for the sheer joy he got from thumping in goals.

But where one door closes another opens. He was offered the job as manager of lowly Hartlepool United and threw himself into that task with all the fire and energy that had made him such a deadly centre-forward.

His first act was to contact his old friend Peter Taylor and ask him to join him. Peter had been Middlesbrough's goalkeeper and the pair had spent hours discussing their ideas on how to run a football club. Now was the chance to put those ideas into practice.

There was little cash available at Hartlepool and Brian and Peter became Jacks-of-all-trades—

• *Focus On*
A Headline-
Maker . . .

THAT MAN CLOUGH!

FOUR FACES OF CLOUGH

AGGRESSIVE!

AT EASE!

ADMONISHING!

AMEN!

☆ ☆ ☆ ☆ ☆ ☆

repairing leaking roofs, humping terracing blocks into place, and touring the area to scrape up money from locals.

On the field, too, they began to develop the push-and–run football that was to become their trademark with Derby and Nottingham.

A 16-year-old Scot, John McGovern, was thrown into the team because he could sort out chaos with one accurate pass.

That has been Brian Clough's hallmark ever since. He asks only that his players use their strengths. That they play and train honestly to the best of their ability.

That is why his teams at Derby and Nottingham have both been so dangerous on the break. They don't hang around on the edge of their own penalty-box. Many a goal has been scored with a flurry of first-time passes that take the opposition by complete surprise.

But a manager has to be much more than a good coach. He has to have the courage and the judgement to buy players.

Throughout his career Brian Clough has never hesitated to spend money to get the player he wants.

When manager of Derby he once threatened to sleep the night in his car outside Archie Gemmill's house if he didn't sign. He was invited to spend the night in a spare bedroom and signed his man over breakfast next morning!

England centre-half Roy McFarland got a midnight knock on his door when the Clough-Taylor combine decided they wanted to sign him from Tranmere Rovers.

The partnership is built on the trust of twenty years of friendship. Peter Taylor is the man who spots the talent. Brian Clough has said he would spend a million pounds on his judgement—and he has already spent well over that figure on his signings so far.

He gambles where so many hesitate. Forest had no money to spend when he took over. But he did not wait to make his money. He went out and signed players like John McGovern, Peter Withe and Larry Lloyd.

When Forest won promotion he spent half a million pounds to sign Peter Shilton, Kenny Burns and Archie Gemmill. And when centre half Larry Lloyd was injured Clough sped down to London to buy Q. P. R.'s Dave Needham as a £140,000 replacement.

The result of all this action has been success. From the 10,000 gates Forest were drawing when Clough arrived, they climbed rapidly towards 45,000 full house occasions.

Brian Clough was widely tipped to take over as England manager but the job went to Ron Greenwood. Instead Clough and Taylor were put in charge of the England under-18 team.

If they do well there they are the hot tips to take over from Greenwood in 1980.

His choice as manager of the youngsters may surprise many who remember his fiery outbursts on T.V. in his stormy days with Derby and a short unhappy time with Leeds United.

But although he is very strict on day-to-day discipline, Brian Clough is a man very much at home with youngsters. His sons Simon and Nigel are often to be seen scampering around his office—or perched on the Forest bench during a match!

He goes along to watch them play for their school teams and has been known to sign a kid for his club from a parks game. Above all he spends much of his time away from football helping to raise funds for handicapped children or visiting them in hospital.

He looked on his job with the England under -18 squad as a chance to help young lads to get the best out of life. To teach them discipline. To do the simple things right.

And above all to have pride in the white jersey of their country.

47

WHOSE FACE BENEATH THE GREASEPAINT?

Hidden beneath the clown's make-up is a Scottish World Cup star. Can you guess who it is?

You should have no problem recognising him from this picture. Yes, it's Alan Rough, Scotland and Partick Thistle goalkeeper.

Although well used to the roar of the crowd it was the smell of greasepaint that lured Alan to the Kelvin Hall Circus in Glasgow.

After five minutes of skilful make-up by another clown, Professor Grimble—it was into the ring to a great roar from the crowd. And the crowd's enjoyment was shared by Alan.

"I love the circus—but I never thought I'd be anything but a spectator. It was fantastic!"

PETER the GREAT!

TWO against one—but PETER BARNES, Manchester City's wizard of the wing, gets in his shot despite the desperate efforts of Arsenal men, PAT RICE, (on left) and JOHN MATTHEWS.

KEEP GOAL

MANCHESTER CITY'S BIG JOE CORRIGAN GIVES THE LOW DOWN ON WHAT MAKES A GOOD GOALIE

IN my view fitness is the most important thing for a goalkeeper who hopes to reach the top.

The reason is simple. A keeper can stand around for 89 minutes with nothing to do. But he has to be ready to explode into action for one vital save. His reflexes must be razor sharp and his muscles strong and tight.

That is why I train even harder than the outfield players at Manchester City.

The next thing is catching. If you can't catch a ball cleanly then forget goalkeeping. You have to be able to hang on to the ball at any angle and under all sorts of pressure from forwards.

If you are a good natural catcher then get to work on the techniques. If you go up for a high catch try to make sure that both thumbs are together behind the ball. If they are not, the ball can slip through.

For lower catches try always to get your body behind the ball as a second defence. Use your chest as a cushion, leaning forward so the ball will not bounce back off you.

Courage is another vital asset for a 'keeper. The game is not all fancy dives. There are times when you have to hurl yourself down among the feet. You can't afford to hesitate. You have to forget that the boot swinging in on the ball has six studs. If you worry about being hurt you will probably get a knock.

There's no substitute for hard work and a goalkeeper is no exception. You may have seen some of my training sessions which were featured on television. They showed a five minute stint where I had shots fired at me first to the left then to the right.

IT'S almost ten years since Joe Corrigan first stepped into Manchester City's goal as a nervous teenager.

He had to face a lot more pressure than most youngsters. For a start his huge 6 ft. 5 in. frame meant that he drew far more attention than the average size player.

Secondly the colourful Malcolm Allison was assistant manager at City in those days. He described young Joe as the " second Frank Swift." Swift was a legendary figure with City fans.

One of the best and most spectacular keepers in the history of the game he had been an England international and a great favourite with older City followers.

When young Joe stepped under the crossbar it was inevitable that he would be compared with the great Swift—and at 18 he had no chance of winning that battle.

Every little mistake was picked on. As the criticism grew—

the harder Joe tried and the more nervous he became.

For a while he had to suffer intense barracking from some of City's fans. At one stage he was on the verge of quitting the game altogether. But he gritted his teeth, threw himself into training even harder and gradually forced his critics to applaud him.

In 1976 he was called up for England duty. Voted "Player of the Year" by the City fans and at last accepted as one of the best goalkeepers in the business. If ever there was an example for youngsters to follow it is big Joe.

CORRIGAN STYLE!

I finished up flat on my back absolutely exhausted.

I can tell you that in a normal work-out that is the second spell of pressure work I would do—and that after an hour and a half of other training.

You need pals to help you out by shooting or crossing the ball. Start on the long range work then build up until you get the ball volleyed from short range.

Stamina is the key factor. You've to be able to pull off a dive or a leap when you are just about all in from a hard match. That is why I teach myself to make saves when every muscle in my body is screaming for a rest.

For young 'keepers catching cleanly is the main thing to worry about. Later on when your team begins to think about tactics you will have to learn to work off your line.

That usually means coming out to catch a cross to help your defenders.

The thing to remember here is never to change your mind once you have made the decision to go. If you are not quite set for the catch you can always punch. If you stop you are in no-man's land.

When going out for a cross try to meet the ball at its highest point. You have the advantage of using arms and hands so the higher the ball is in the air the less chance your opponents have of outjumping you.

So get your mates to sling over a few crosses and learn to judge where the ball will be at its highest point when it passes across your goal.

Gloves and caps are equipment which goalkeepers use by their own choice. If it makes you feel better, use it—that's the rule. I always tape my gloves to wrist. If they are not taped and get wet and heavy there is a fair chance that you will find them slipping down your hands. That way the ball and gloves can land in the back of the net.

I always take a cap out with me but never wear it. You don't often play directly into the sun so it's not that much of a help. On the other hand if it falls off as you go for a ball it can take your eye off the ball.

Finally I would say that a young goalkeeper must learn to accept the loneliness of the job. When you make a mistake there is nothing you can do about it. You can't chase upfield and score a goal to make up. You are stuck there in your goal and maybe the crowd are shouting at you.

You must have the character to take it. You must learn not to worry about mistakes or you will lose concentration and probably make another error. That can be the hardest thing of all.

Normally I would advise youngsters to try all the outfield positions before they think about goalkeeping. But if you want to be a 'keeper then you will have to start thinking about all I have said—and a whole lot more. It's a tough job—but it's great to be a goalkeeper.

It's hard work being a professional footballer but Joe Corrigan always has time to meet youngsters like nine-year-old Patrick Bailey.

IAN WALLACE, Coventry City

HIGH-RISE RIMMER

"THAT BALL'S MINE!"—
That's the clear message from JIMMY RIMMER, Aston Villa goalkeeper.

ALL IN A HURRY!

PETER EASTOE, Q.P.R.

STEVE HEIGHWAY, Liverpool.

MARTIN O'NEILL, Nottingham Fores[t]

DAVE THOMAS,
Everton, (white shorts)
and PHIL NEAL,
Liverpool.

JOHN BRAMHALL,
Tranmere Rovers.

STAN BOWLES,
Q.P.R.

KEN SANSOM,
Crystal Palace.

THE MAGIC OF DARK BLUE

by *Tom Forsyth*

HE WEARS THE LIGHT BLUE OF RANGERS

" J AWS ", that's the name by which the fans have come to know me. Tommy Docherty, when he was manager of Manchester United, had another ' pet ' name for me, too. To him I was a " Clydesdale " in comparison to Martin Buchan.

In other words, I've got a reputation for being the big bad wolf of Scottish football.

But I wonder if those who invented, and chant, these nick-names know that Tom Forsyth, the so-called ' Iron Man ' of Rangers and Scotland, was once so small and thin he became his local amateur club's mascot.

And that for many years was the closest I ever got to football —watching the bigger fellows playing.

Born in Paisley, I lived there for only two years, before our family moved to Stonehouse, and I've remained there ever since.

But my earliest recollections are of always having a ball at my feet, little nipper though I was.

Then when the local junior side, Stonehouse Violet, packed up and an amateur team, Stone- house Thistle, grew up in their place, I got the job as mascot and number one ball-boy. I'd be eight or nine at that time.

Looking back, it was a big help watching the older lads in action.

But I won't say it helped me set the world alight as a school- boy footballer. I simply plodded along in the school team.

The highlight of those days,

came when Stonehouse asked me to play when they were a couple of men short one Saturday. What a game that was!

Our opponents needed only two points to win the League title.

We had trouble in raising a full team so one of the linesmen, who just happened to be an official of the team we were playing, made up the numbers for us.

As the game went on however, we noticed this fellow kept on ' mistakenly ' passing the ball to one of our opponents.

It was so bad we told him to clear off and finished the match with only ten men.

In the end, we were beaten two goals to one, giving our opponents the championship.

My other memory of that game is being put through with only their goalkeeper to beat. He was about twice my size, unfortunately, and knocked me out cold when we clashed!

Even when I was asked to join Glenavon, another amateur club from my hometown area, at the age of 16, I still wasn't sure I had any chance of making the grade as a footballer.

But as that side grew up together, they went from strength to strength.

In 1967 we went to London to play a challenge match against a Crystal Palace team at Selhurst Park. We gave them a 5-1 drubbing.

The next day, on top of the world, we watched Scotland beat England 3-2 at Wembley. The first country to beat them since they'd won the World Cup a year earlier.

As I watched the after-the- -match invasion of the pitch by

WEMBLEY DREAM THAT CAME TRUE

Scots fans, I knew I had to try to become a professional and aim for the honour of wearing a dark blue jersey one day.

But there were to be a couple of false starts on the road to wearing that dark blue jersey.

Dundee United were the first club to offer me a trial, I remember. I stayed overnight in Dundee and played a full-scale practice game at Tannadice, United's ground, in the morning. But I obviously failed to impress Jerry Kerr, who was manager then, for I was never asked back.

Partick Thistle were next in line, but once again my display in a trial game at Firhill failed to persuade Thistle's management that I was worth signing.

However, my next trial for my nearest senior club, Motherwell, proved to be third time lucky.

Bobby Howitt was then manager at Fir Park, and he allowed me to remain a part-timer while I finished my apprenticeship as a joiner.

Just as well, too. It was the only thing that was putting any muscle on my skinny little frame at that time!

Mind you, it's lucky I was a fit young man, too, for combining work with play was a real strain, I can tell you.

There were nights when I almost crawled out of Fir Park and made it home to bed.

Unfortunately, this wasn't the best of periods for Motherwell, either. At the end of my first season in 1968, we were relegated to the Second Division.

On looking back, relegation may have been a blessing in disguise.

It not only allowed the team time to regroup and come back with fresh confidence, but youngsters like myself got a real chance to establish ourselves.

I scored quite a few of the goals which won us the championship the following season, because Bobby Howitt fancied me as a striker. I managed to notch 18 goals.

In the First Division, though, being a defender became my more natural game. And it was as a defender that I won my first international cap against Denmark—and then the thing I'd

always dreamt of—a transfer to Rangers.

Two days after leaving Motherwell, I was back playing against them—in a Rangers jersey!

That didn't bother me. I'm just not the worrying kind!

I don't even care that I've been called "Jaws" or been compared to a Clydesdale.

Winning matches for my team and playing football to the best of my ability is what concerns me. Not what people think.

I will admit, though, that I do experience an entirely different sensation whenever I play for Scotland.

For me, it's an indescribable feeling when you pull on the dark blue jersey.

Ten years after I'd seen Scotland beat England in 1967, I played my first full match at Wembley and finished on the winning side. It was a dream come true.

So what's left in the future for me?

At club level, to repeat our recent success all over again. I have four championship medals already. More will always be welcome.

Another highlight of my career was scoring the winning goal in a Scottish Cup final.

It was against Celtic at the end of my first full season at Ibrox, in 1973.

With the score at 2-2 a Derek Johnstone header rebounded from the post straight to my feet.

It seemed like a certain goal.

But I'd run in so quickly to cheer the winning goal, thinking the ball had already crossed the line, that I had to drag my leg backwards to make contact—and I didn't even do that properly. But they all count, don't they?

As to what I'll do when my playing days are all over, that's something I've no intention of even thinking about just yet.

I've got years of football left in me, and not until I actually have to stop playing will I consider whether or not I want to stay in the game as a coach or manager.

Perhaps if I do become a manager, people will start calling me "Mr Jaws"—you never know!

DEREK JOHNSTONE —a vital header.

Away from it all!

DAVE NEEDHAM, Nottingham Forest stalwart defender, finds the country life the way to unwind after the pressures of big-time football.

Dave reckons that coping with the livestock at his Market Bosworth home is an easy task compared to keeping tabs on football's top strikers.

Dave Needham joined Nottingham Forest only six months after leaving Forest's neighbours, Notts County. He had made over 450 appearances for County before Queen's Park Rangers signed him for £80,000.

Then after a few months, Brian Clough pounced—and Dave was a Forest player.

Five-year-old Dominic lends his dad a helping hand.

Calling in the cows.

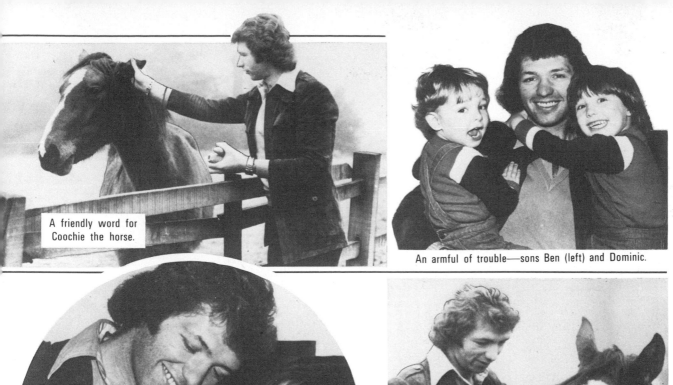

A friendly word for Coochie the horse.

An armful of trouble—sons Ben (left) and Dominic.

Dave with wife, Jacky, and baby Demelsa.

Coochie makes short work of his favourite tit-bit—carrots.

Early morning—Dave checks on the animals before leaving for a training stint.

60   **MIKE WALSH, Bolton Wanderers**

STEVE BUCKLEY, Derby County

61

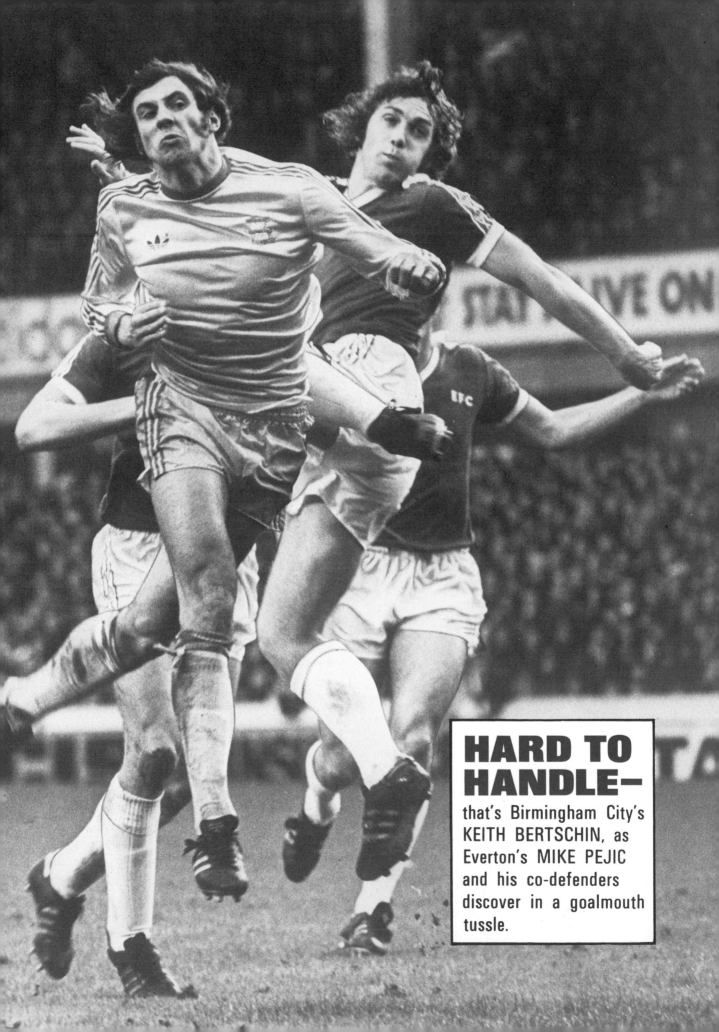

HARD TO HANDLE–

that's Birmingham City's KEITH BERTSCHIN, as Everton's MIKE PEJIC and his co-defenders discover in a goalmouth tussle.

HE SAID "Sign here," please, 10,000 TIMES!

A PICTURE in a football magazine over 35 years ago started a Sheffield man on a hunt that has taken him the length and breadth of the country.

When Sheffield Wednesday supporter David Williams took the photograph of his idol, the late Jackie Robinson, down to Hillsborough to have it autographed, little did he know that one day he would be able to boast one of the finest collections of football pictures in the country!

For that single photo has now "snowballed" into a massive library of over 10,000 personally autographed snaps of footballers spanning the past 35 years.

" I don't think there is a player you could name in the forties, fifties and sixties whom I haven't met," says Mr Williams.

The collection is now neatly indexed and catalogued in a bureau in Mr Williams' house in Sheffield.

Mr Williams can recollect years of waiting outside hotels and grounds . . . sometimes until late into the evening.

" I've got all the greats of the past such as Matthews and Finney and all the Manchester United victims in the Munich air disaster. But the most treasured is that of Jackie Robinson. He is now dead but I will never forget him."

" During the years I became friendly with the commissionaires at hotels and they used to tip me off as to who was staying there.

" Once I was waiting for the Hull City players outside a hotel and their manager, former England player Raich Carter, invited me to travel to the ground on the team coach with them. That was a great moment for me.

" I didn't just get the players in Sheffield hotels. I've travelled from as far south as Southampton to up north in Sunderland and from the west at Blackpool to as far east as Grimsby."

The collection has also enabled Mr Williams to strike up friendships with former favourites such as ex-Newcastle United player George Robledo—who scored the winning goal for the Magpies in the 1952 Cup final against Arsenal.

" That started when I bumped into him in the street. A friend who was with me happened to have a camera with him and I took the snap myself," Mr Williams recalls.

" After that meeting we gradually got to know

DAVID WILLIAMS CAN PICTURE IT ALL!

each other. We started writing and also sent each other Christmas cards."

But the most patient story came when Mr Williams tried to get the autograph of a cricketer!

" I waited ages for Len Hutton's autograph. He was Yorkshire and England's skipper and opening bat. I missed him before he went on to the ground and he was in the field all day.

" I finally caught up with him as he was walking out to bat. He had his batting gloves on but still managed to sign the picture."

Although Mr Williams no longer does much work on the collection, there is one player he would like to get.

" Johan Cruyff's is the only autograph I have missed that I would have liked for my collection," says Mr Williams.

63

'KEEPERS IN CLOSE-UP

1. **PAT JENNINGS**
   Arsenal
2. **PHIL PARKES**
   Q.P.R.
3. **RAY CLEMENCE**
   Liverpool
4. **JOHN PHILLIPS**
   Chelsea
5. **PETER SHILTON**
   Nottingham Forest
6. **BARRY SIDDALL**
   Sunderland

HUNGRY FOR GOALS!

"**D**IXIE" was my nickname when I first joined Aston Villa as a teenager. Not because I looked likely to match the famous 'Dixie' Dean's scoring feats with Everton in the 1930's. It was just because our surnames are similar.

But I reckon my goal record in European games for Villa and the England Under-21 side last term would have done the original 'Dixie' proud.

At club level I notched five goals in seven U.E.F.A. Cup games while for Young England I hit four in three matches.

Dixie Dean's amazing record of sixty League goals in a season will never be repeated. Last term Everton centre-forward Bob Latchford won rave reviews by scoring half as many.

But I'm developing a taste for goals. I can sense where and when the opening will occur. And that is the major reason for me progressing from the Villa reserve side to the full England squad within three years.

I owe a great deal to Villa manager Ron Saunders and the Under-21 boss Dave Sexton.

Dave is, of course, also manager of Manchester United but that doesn't prevent him generating enthusiasm and ideas when the Under-21's meet up for games.

Both Mr Saunders and Mr Sexton understand and enjoy working with their strikers. Goal-scoring comes naturally to me but it's great working with managers who encourage your team-mates to give you the best service in the penalty-area.

ASTON VILLA STRIKER, JOHN DEEHAN, TELLS HIS STORY

Dave Sexton is especially good at planning set moves. That makes a corner or a free-kick dangerous and not just a hopeful ball into the penalty area.

Playing with the Under-21's has convinced me England have a bright international future.

The competition for places is fierce. But there are so many really skilful players around. Lads like Arsenal's Graham Rix, Spurs' Glenn Hoddle, Southampton's Steve Williams and Bolton's Peter Reid have all been battling for midfield places. Yes, you can see all of them having a bright career in the full England set-up.

When you add to those names forwards like Peter Barnes and Tony Woodcock, who have already won senior caps, you realise the talent emerging in England.

I'm just grateful now that I made the right decision three years ago. A decision that could have cost me my England future.

66

"I'VE HAD MY SET - BACKS"

Under the parentage rule I could have played for Eire. When I first came through with Villa that was the country many folk tried to persuade me to play for.

I used to do a lot of work for the Irish clubs around Birmingham and as a token of thanks they bought me a set of golf clubs. They also brought Eire manager Johnny Giles along to make the presentation. At the time he was player-boss of West Bromwich Albion.

Johnny asked me to play for Eire and I was aware I was more likely to win full caps quickly and travel the world if I gave him the nod.

But Ron Saunders told me he thought I would play for England one day. Also that I was close to an Under-21 call-up. How right he was.

Another young forward has made his name with Eire of course. Arsenal's Frank Stapleton. And it's amazing to think five years ago the Gunners wanted to sign me to play alongside Frank in their youth team.

As a schoolboy Villa had watched me a few times. But it was only when they heard Arsenal were ready to step in that they made a move.

The Villa scouts told my dad if I went down to London for trials I'd never come back. Arsenal would easily persuade me that Highbury was the place for me.

I don't think my parents fancied the idea of me being near the bright lights when I was so young. A month's trial at Villa Park was quickly arranged.

And after just one week I was signed as an apprentice professional!

In many ways I suppose I've shot to the top, but I've also had my set-backs.

It was heartbreaking to be knocked out in the quarter-finals of last year's U.E.F.A. Cup by Barcelona.

In the first leg at Villa Park, Dutch star Johan Cruyff had a blinder until he limped off in the second half. He was at the hub of all the Spanish team's moves and helped them into a two-nil lead.

It was only our guts and determination that brought us back into the tie –Ken McNaught and myself scoring late goals to make the second leg a real battle.

In Spain even though we had full back John Gidman sent off early in the game we snatched a first-half goal to go ahead 3—2 on aggregate.

RON SAUNDERS
— how right he was!

But in the second half we cracked and let two goals in. Our European hopes were ended.

Even though we won the 1977 League Cup final against Everton I still look on our first meeting with them at Wembley as a major disappointment.

After two replays we eventually came out on top. But in front of 100,000 fans at Wembley we played out a boring 0-0 draw. How I wish I could have found my scoring boots that day!

But I was more than pleased to pick up a winners medal, my greatest club honour to date.

I have no doubt about what rates as my greatest international honour. That has to be my first ever call-up to the full England side for last season's match against Brazil.

The big game was on a Wednesday night and on the Monday I had to play for Villa against Newcastle. I had a terrible game against the Geordies.

My mind was really miles away from Villa Park—at Wembley!

I couldn't concentrate on a League game when I was due to face the famous Brazil.

Fortunately we beat Newcastle and everyone was happy to wish me all the best for the international.

I only sat on the substitutes' bench whilst the England lads were given a rough ride by the South Americans. But I felt involved and really wanted by England boss Ron Greenwood.

Youngsters often ask me for advice about playing up-front. But I reckon the best thing they can learn is not to become depressed if they miss easy chances.

Andy Gray, Bob Latchford, Trevor Francis and the rest have all missed their share of 'sitters'.

When Villa beat Ipswich 6-1 last season an Andy Gray effort came down off the cross-bar and I had an empty net. It was a certain goal. Guess what? I headed it 'way over the top!

The crowd couldn't believe it. It must have looked terrible. But I didn't lose my confidence. Within minutes I was in the air to power a header into the net from a difficult angle. A great goal.

And that illustrates how a striker can be feeling down-in-the-dumps one minute but must be ready to snap up a chance the next.

DAVE SEXTON
— ideas and enthusiasm

UP-AND OVER!

GEOFF MERRICK of Bristol City is the high-flyer — LEIGHTON JAMES, Q.P.R., is the springboard.

KIDOLOGY CAN COUNT — TOMMY CAVANAGH TELLS HOW

WHEREVER they play, Manchester United's fame and glamour draw the fans in their thousands. The team has always had its share of international stars and that is still true today.

It seems only right that they should be coached and encouraged by a man who is himself a larger-than-life character. Crowds immediately recognise the silver-haired figure of Tommy Cavanagh when he sprints over to treat an injured player.

The top names in football recognise him, too, and have always been eager to employ his services. In fact this Englishman born in Liverpool has been trainer to both the Scottish and Irish international sides.

He worked with the Scots when Tommy Docherty had a spell in charge of the international team. He is still with Northern Ireland having been asked to take the job by their manager, Danny Blanchflower.

" I am always delighted to work with footballers whatever country they represent," Tommy says.

" I have been lucky to work and play with some of the biggest names in the game. Now that I am at Old Trafford I can put a lifetime of experience into the job.

" Like everyone else in this game I have known the ups and downs. There are so few winners in any one season, most of the time you are battling against disappointment of some sort.

" That is where the coach becomes so important. On a Monday morning after you have lost, the job is to lift the players back into the mood for hard work.

" You don't do that by snarling or threatening. You have to get the smiles back and that means hiding your own disappointment and bouncing into the dressing-room making them feel that next Saturday they will murder the opposition.

" Confidence is so much to do with success in football and even the little things help.

" I have a routine each match day when I get the team list of our opponents. I take it into the United dressing-room while the players are changing. I have a quick look at the players on the list then tear it up and throw it in the waste-paper basket saying, ' What a load of rubbish—we'll walk this lot '.

" That's rarely true in the First Division but the lads like a bit of kidology like that.

" I have been in the game as a player and coach for over thirty years.

" People never think about trainers as part of a team but I can assure you they can get as nervous as the players.

" I remember my very first game on the bench with the bucket and sponge. There wasn't a single injury for 89 minutes. I was desperate to get out there and show my worth.

" When a player eventually went down I charged across the pitch like a greyhound. It was only when I reached the injured player I found I had forgotten the magic sponge!

" Referees too can get caught up in the atmosphere of a big game. I went on to treat a United player who had a very painful leg injury. When I got to him the crowd were already whistling and shouting for the game to restart.

" The ref yelled at me to get him straight off the pitch as it wasn't a serious injury. I asked when he had qualified as a doctor! I was angry at the time, but I soon realised that the ref was like the rest of us—tensed up and anxious to keep the game going.

" You tend to forget that a referee also has 50,000 or more fans roaring at him. I try to have a joke to relax the tension.

" I have been privileged to work with some of the great players down the years.

" People are very critical of footballers. But to make it to the very top you need a tremendous amount of hard work, great skill and the nerve to use it in front of a huge crowd.

" It's tough but if you have the passion and love for the game it can be a wonderful life."

ANDY GRAY, Aston Villa

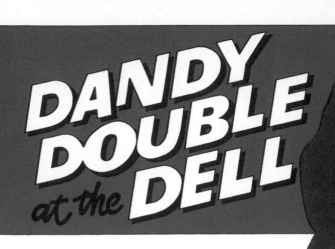

DANDY DOUBLE at the DELL

YOU'VE heard of the " loneliness of the long-distance runner." Well, in my case it's the " happiness of the long-distance runner."

I was in the cross-country team at school, and I have always enjoyed running.

I must be one of the few footballers who enjoys a cross-country training run!

My ability to keep running for ninety minutes—allied to some football skill, of course—has brought me one England cap and a couple of big money transfers.

But it also made me the perfect foil for the finishing skills of Ted MacDougall—and my partnership with Ted is really the story of my career.

Ted MacDougall and I have played together for York City, Bournemouth, Norwich City and Southampton.

Ted has scored most of the goals while I have supplied many of the crosses and passes.

His sharpness in the box and eye for a chance have blended with my stamina and pace. It was a blend that seemed to work from our first game at York.

Ted has won caps for Scotland, and I have my one

TED MACDOUGALL — sharpshooter

Bond sensed that we had a special kind of understanding on the field.

He really worked at it. We spent hours training and perfecting moves. John Bond taught us so much more about football.

Dummy runs, decoys, cross-over runs. All aimed at creating space for Ted to use his sharpness.

Always I knew when Ted would head for the near post or the far post, and exactly what kind of pass he wanted.

Southampton's Phil Boyer tells how it all began.

for England. Without our partnership I don't believe either of us would have reached international level.

It's just a pity we were not both English (or Scottish).

It all began a long time ago at York. Ted MacDougall had failed to make his mark at Liverpool, and moved to York for about £4,000.

I hadn't impressed at Derby, and joined York for a similar fee to Ted's.

We had an understanding from the start. I seemed to know just where Ted was going to be when I hit my crosses.

Then Tom Johnston took over as manager from Joe Shaw, and moved me into the middle alongside Ted. From then our partnership developed Between us we hit 28 goals in the season—19 to Ted, 9 for me.

We were split up for a season when John Bond bought Ted for £10,000 for Bournemouth. But Ted mentioned me to John and I followed him south next season for around £20,000.

That's when our partnership really took off. John

We reached near perfection in one match—an F.A. Cup tie against Margate.

Every time we attacked we seemed liable to score. The final result was 11—0—and Ted claimed nine of them.

Ted's nine goals are still a record for the F.A. Cup. He could have cracked the all-time British record of 13 with a bit of luck.

All this was attracting a lot of attention. Eventually Ted was bought by Manchester United, before moving to West Ham, and then to Norwich City, where he linked up again with John Bond.

Once John had Ted at Carrow Road he wanted to pair us up again.

But there were problems. He'd already taken Bournemouth players Mel Machin, John Benson and Tony Powell, in addition to coach Fred Davies and assistant manager Ken Brown. And John Bond himself, of course, had joined Norwich from Bournemouth.

The south coast club were not in the mood to transfer any more players to Norwich, so although I

DISAPPOINTING DAY AT WEMBLEY

was available for transfer, it didn't look as if I was going to link up with Ted MacDougall again.

Then Bournemouth arranged a transfer to Chelsea for £100,000. The deal was all set up. I went to London and had talks with manager Dave Sexton.

All it needed was for me to say ' yes '.

But back came John Bond. He offered an extra £45,000 and that did the trick. I was a Norwich player, and able to link up with Ted again.

After a couple of full seasons together at Carrow Road, Ted joined Southampton, and a few months later I followed him again.

Once more I could have joined a London club. Both Arsenal and Queen's Park Rangers wanted me.

But Lawrie McMenemy impressed me so much with his determination to build a First Division club at the Dell, that the prospect of joining forces with Ted was only a part of my decision to sign for the Saints.

I feel my career has been given a fresh look at the Dell. Playing with people like Peter Osgood (before he went to America), Alan Ball and Chris Nicholl has taught me a lot.

NEEDLE MATCH

I still hope to get back into the England international squads if we can get a good run in the First Division with Southampton.

In fact I'm still rather wondering why I was left out after my first international appearance! I played my one and only senior international against Wales at Wrexham in the Welsh ' Centenary ' match.

We won 2—1, and I felt I did my job. Working hard off the ball, and trying to use it well when I had the ball.

But Don Revie, then the England team manager, never said a word to me afterwards.

That is one of the big disappointments of my career. To feel you've played well and not get another chance is quite a blow.

The other big disappointment was the League Cup Final of 1975 when Norwich City played Aston Villa in an all-Second Division final.

There was quite a bit of " needle " in the match—partly because we were rivals for promotion and partly because Villa's manager, Ron Saunders, was previously in charge at Norwich.

We lost 1-0, but it was not the result that was so disappointing.

It was the way we played. We didn't show our real ability. John Bond had built a side that could play skilful football, but we didn't show any of it at Wembley.

My only memory of the match is of big Chris Nicholl—now my team-mate at the Dell—dominating in the air and nodding away every single cross we hit.

We " froze " on the day, never relaxing enough to produce our normal attacking style.

All we could do was pump high balls into the Villa penalty-box, and big Chris

was happy to head them away all day and all night if necessary.

I will always cherish the experience of playing in a Wembley final—but I wish we had played better.

I'd like to think I could go back there with Southampton and do myself justice.

Everything is geared to success at the Dell. Off the field the set-up could hardly be better. A splendid gymnasium at the ground, very good facilities for supporters.

CONFIDENCE BOOST

There's a good blend of experience and youth in the side, with some top-class youngsters waiting to break through.

Despite my success in the past in partnership with Ted MacDougall, I feel the next year or two could be the best yet.

At least I have overcome the groin injury that threatened my career at Norwich. For six months I never kicked a ball, and I had to stay in bed for six weeks.

When I got up the pain was still there! I thought I was never going to get rid of it. I was offered the chance of an operation. It meant grafting some bone from the hip into the groin, and there was only a fifty-fifty chance of success. If it failed that was it—no more football. I declined the offer and relied on daily physiotherapy. Every day after training I went for treatment. Sometimes twice a day for an hour a time.

Gradually the injury got better, until I could train without pain. I had not played a competitive match for several months and wondered just how I would shape up. But then Southampton made an offer for me, which Norwich accepted.

It was the best confidence boost I could have. A medical check complete with X-rays proved there was nothing more to worry about.

I'm looking forward to running a lot further yet creating goals for somebody—and scoring a few myself.

LAWRIE McMENEMY — determined on success

CHRIS NICHOLL — dominating in the air

PHIL BOYER, Southampton

JOHN MAHONEY, Middlesbrough

JIM MONTGOMERY RECALLS...
"My moment of Wembley glory"

MAY 5th 1973. Nothing special about that date for most people. But to me it is still as vivid today as it was when I strode out on to Wembley Stadium.

The match was the F.A. Cup final between Sunderland and Leeds United. I was in goal for Sunderland that day when we pulled off one of the great shocks in Wembley history.

We were in the Second Division while Leeds were one of the most powerful outfits in the First and odds-on favourites to take the cup.

And yet the score at the end of ninety minutes was Sunderland 1 Leeds United 0 and there were scenes of joy at the end.

Sunderland fans had been starved of success and the atmosphere at Wembley that afternoon was electric. With 50,000 roaring ' Sunderland ' it was like waves of thunder rolling out over the pitch.

My moment of glory came in the second-half. Ian Porterfield had put us one up and we were hanging on grimly as Leeds came storming back.

Then Trevor Cherry got clear on the left side of goal for a header I just managed to parry across goal. I was on my knees as it rolled to Peter Lorimer two yards out. He has the hardest shot in the game and he let rip. It was instinct that dragged me up off the ground to hurl myself across the goal line.

I got my left hand in the path of the shot and the ball flew up against the bar and rebounded to safety.

I have a video tape of that save and I often watch it and think Lorimer is bound to score—but I keep getting that hand in the way!

I have many wonderful memories of Sunderland. I was a local lad and made my first team debut at 17. When the team is doing well there is no place like Roker Park for crowd noise.

It was there I played with one of the finest defenders I have ever seen. Charlie Hurley was our centre-half. An Irishman with a Cockney accent!

But he could play. At 6 ft. 1 in. and 14 stone he was almost unbeatable in the air. And when he went forward for a corner-kick the roar of expectation used to start as he crossed the halfway line.

He would keep running and as the kick came over he would take off in a huge leap and smash ferocious headers at the goal. He scored some beauties in his time. For all his power I don't remember Charlie being involved in one bad foul. He was a great sportsman.

I thought I would play out my career with Sunderland.

But then there was a change of management and I was dropped into the reserves. After so many years in the atmosphere of first team football I took that very hard.

But last season Birmingham City stepped in and signed me. Their manager at that time was Willie Bell and I will always be grateful to him for giving me a second chance in the game.

"NO PLACE LIKE ROKER PARK"

I have loved it at St Andrew's. Since Jim Smith took over from Sir Alf Ramsey as manager, we have really started to put some results together. He is a very straight talking boss so you know exactly what he wants from the team.

I believe the crowds will be packing St Andrew's before long to see the football they have long waited to cheer.

I think they will get it, too, because we have the player I regard as the best forward in the country. I had played for Sunderland against Trevor Francis. I rated him highly then.

Now I am playing behind him in the same team I can only say he is the most exciting attacker in football. He has pace, he is always in control of the ball, he has a fierce and accurate shot and most important of all he is a team player. We have a lot of other good players but this lad is special.

If he gets the support of a winning team around him the fans will be climbing the walls to see him.

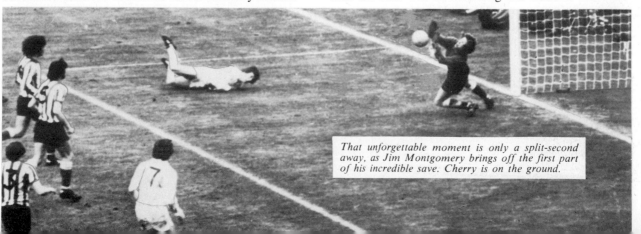

That unforgettable moment is only a split-second away, as Jim Montgomery brings off the first part of his incredible save. Cherry is on the ground.

MICK DROY

Chelsea

DON GIVENS

Queen's Park Rangers

THE GREIG COLLECTION

A CHESTFUL of medals is the hallmark of top service chiefs like Earl Mountbatten (below).

But footballers, too, are no slouches at medal-gathering. John Greig of Rangers shows how his medals would look if displayed on his jacket. Proof of a long and successful football career that now sees him as manager at Ibrox.

Every medal hard won in football's toughest competitions—and highly valued by John. After this picture was taken the medals were packed away and returned for safe-keeping to the bank.

He once " lost " two medals after his collection was loaned out. Now the medals remain in the strong-room in the bank.

How the medals are laid out:-

The left side of the jacket, that is on right of picture, is headed by the M.B.E. Below it a group of four S.F.A. International medals.

On each lapel are the square medals from U.E.F.A., on left, the Cup Winner's Cup medal when Rangers beat Moscow Dynamo in Barcelona (1972), and on right, the Runner-up medal in the same competition when Bayern Munich won (1967).

Below the U.E.F.A. medal, is a row of eight League International medals. Beneath the S.F.A. group of medals are, in line abreast, five Scottish Cup Winner medals then seven League Cup medals. Below, the next line, four First Division or Premier League medals.

Next two Glasgow Cup medals with, below them, the single medal, the first John ever won—an Edinburgh Schools medal. On the extreme right is the large silver commemorative medal given after a Rangers v. Vancouver match in the year of the Canadian Olympics.

Finally, the bottom line, are two more Schools medals and two Juvenile medals.

In his hand, John holds four Olympic Commemorative medals from Canada.

SKATES INSTEAD OF BOOTS

The Day The Pitch Became A Rink

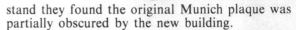

EVERY football club's ground has something which makes it special. Just a little thing perhaps—a plaque, a clock, part of the terracing—but something which is all part of the club's history and tradition.

For instance the Anfield Kop must rate as one of the most famous sections of terracing in the world.

On its steeply-banked slopes 24,000 Merseysiders sing their Liverpool idols to success on the field far below.

The Kop's correct title is Spion Kop. That was a commanding hill in Natal captured from the Boers by General Buller in 1900 during the relief of Ladysmith.

Other League grounds have their own Spion Kops—Blackpool and Sheffield Wednesday, for instance—but to most fans there is only one Kop . . . at Liverpool.

Manchester United have their own Kop equivalent in the Stretford End. But when it comes to legends United's three Munich memorials take precedence.

In February, 1958, eight United players died in an air disaster at Munich. Afterwards a clock and a plaque which was cast in the shape of a football ground were placed on the walls of Old Trafford.

Those two tributes to the men who were killed have been seen by fans from all over the world.

But when United built on an addition to their stand they found the original Munich plaque was partially obscured by the new building.

So a new plaque—on the same lines as the first—was produced. That can now be seen in a prominent position outside the new Warwick Road stand.

Ground development was also responsible for the partial concealment of Sheffield United's most distinctive landmark.

The old cricket pavilion, once used by Yorkshire in county matches, now lies hidden behind a massive cantilever stand.

The county and the football club had shared the ground for more than 80 years. But in the early seventies, United decided to end the oddity of having a three-sided ground and cricket had to go.

Everton also have an "intrusion" into their Goodison Park stadium. A church stands in one corner of the ground. The new stand, built around 1970, had to be finished off short because of it.

It seems that whatever ground developments are made at Goodison in the future, the church will have to stay.

Halifax Town's distinctive feature is the speedway track which encloses the playing area at the Shay.

Crowds on speedway nights exceed the Saturday afternoon football attendances.

Halifax, incidentally, can boast that another sport has taken place on their pitch.

During the big freeze-up of 1963, the club turned the ground into an ice-skating rink. They opened it to the public at 2s 6d while pop records were played over the loud-speakers.

In Victorian times Aston Villa's ground also held a skating rink. In fact there are still traces of the old buildings at Villa Park which housed the rink . . . and a boating lake, aquarium and tropical gardens!

London clubs, too, have their share of legends.

Chelsea have kept the weather cock that stood on their old stand. When the new stand was built, the weathercock, a figure of a famous forward of bygone years, George Hilsdon, was tucked away in a store-room.

Charlton have a turnstile named after Sam Bartram, their goalkeeper who made a record 583 appearances for the club between 1934 and 1956.

These are some of the ways in which football clubs cherish their history and traditions.

The new plaque at Old Trafford.

PETER WARD, Brighton

TONY CURRIE, Leeds United

FIRST DIVISION —I'll make it yet!

WREXHAM GOAL-ACE, DIXIE McNEIL, MAKES A VOW.

WHEN Wrexham clinched promotion to the Second Division last season, I picked up my second Third Division Championship medal and once again moved a step nearer to that, so far, elusive Division One.

I've had fourteen years in football, won those two titles with Wrexham and Hereford United, been top goalscorer in the Football League twice and had seven transfers. But to play in the top flight remains my big ambition.

Although I'm now 31 I haven't given up hope yet And if eventually I do have to hang up my boots without having played in the First Division, I will just look back and think how lucky I was to have made football my life in the first place.

Lucky—because at the age of 20 I was so fed up with League soccer I turned my back on it completely!

I had been in the game three years. I started off with Leicester City who were then in the First Division. They had just been to an FA Cup Final and had a very settled first team. I never progressed beyond the reserves and finally they gave me a free transfer.

82

BOBBY SHINTON
— who is another Wrexham star with his eyes on the First Division

WREXHAM ON THE WAY UP?

Exeter City, who had just been relegated to the Fourth Division, snapped me up in 1966.

The average age of the side was only 20, so we did well to finish the season about halfway up the table. I also ended up as the Club's top scorer with 11 goals.

However, our manager was sacked three quarters way through the season. Then at the end the directors decided to give everyone a free transfer!

I was absolutely shocked. I had been top scorer and yet I had picked up my second free transfer. At the time I was so disillusioned I felt that if this was how a professional footballer was treated then I should opt out.

I did just that. Although I knew I was good enough for the Football League I decided to get a job and play part-time for Corby Town in the Southern League.

I was two seasons with Corby Town and managed to notch over fifty goals for them. I was also really enjoying my football. But Northampton made a £5,000 bid for me. Here was a chance to go back into the League and prove myself. So I took it.

It was in that Northampton side that I really felt I could score a bit. They were a free flowing lot and I managed 33 goals with them.

Two seasons at the County Ground and I was on the move again. In 1972 a £10,000 transfer took me to Lincoln City.

Two and a half years and 53 goals later I was packing my bags again preparing for a £20,000 deal that saw me join the League's newest club . . . Hereford United.

DISAPPOINTMENT

Hereford had been in the League only three seasons when I joined them. But already they were in the Third Division. I finished my first term with them as the League's highest scorer with 31. A year later when Hereford climbed into the Second Division. I hit the net 35 times.

However, Hereford didn't really have the money to strengthen the side and they were relegated in the next season. That remains one of the biggest disappointments of my career.

Finally, at the beginning of season 1977—78, I left Edgar Street in a £67,000 transfer to Wrexham.

As soon as I arrived at the Racecourse Ground I sensed that Wrexham could really go places. How right I was!

We won the Third Division Championship, went to the quarter-final of the League Cup and reached the sixth round of the F.A. Cup. We knocked out Newcastle and Bristol City (twice) and were eventually only stopped by Liverpool and Arsenal. Then we qualified for Europe by winning the Welsh Cup.

The one thing that pleased me most was the fact I scored and played well against First Division opposition.

I also finished the FA Cup campaign as the tournament's top scorer with eleven goals.

Even a great season like that wasn't without its disappointments. Whilst the rest of the lads were finally clinching the Third Division title with a 7-1 hammering of Rotherham United, I had to watch from the sidelines and limp round on crutches on the lap of honour with my leg in plaster.

I had been out for about five weeks because I had damaged my heel. The day before the Rotherham match the doctor decided my foot should be in plaster.

The season went a bit flat for me there. Whilst everyone else was celebrating promotion I didn't quite feel as involved as I would have liked.

It also put a damper on two other targets I had set myself. When last term started I had my sights on bringing my senior total to the two hundred goal mark. Before every season I always aim for 20 goals. It was going to need something like 30 plus to get the 200. When I got to 28 with about two months of the season left I was looking to something more like 40 goals.

DIXIE McNEIL
— happy days at Hereford

But the injury put an end to all that and I fell short of the mark. It would have been a great achievement to finish as the Football League's top scorer three seasons out of the last four!

There's a saying a manager will pay money for someone who can score goals. It was certainly that in my case. Despite the two free transfers, total layout for my services is just over the £100,000 mark. When you consider the money being paid these days it's not a bad price for a return of close on 200 goals.

Sometimes, I look back on my fourteen years and seven moves and wish that I had stayed with the one club. Deciding which club that would have been is a difficult question.

I feel that I have still got four very good years in me. I can't honestly see this Wrexham side going straight back down into the Third Division as Hereford did . . so I might still make it to the First Division.

STRIKER STOPPER

MALCOLM MACDONALD, *Arsenal*

STEVE SIMS, *Leicester*

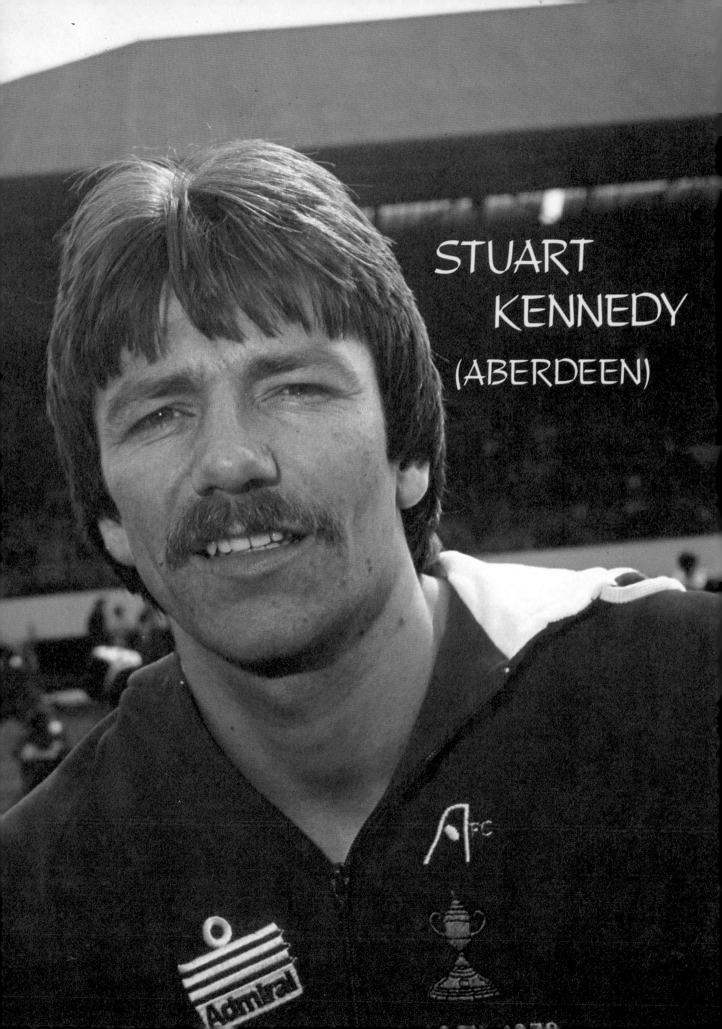

STUART
KENNEDY
(ABERDEEN)

86   **JIMMY MANN,** Bristol City

THE RACE IS ON!

BRIAN ROBERTS, Coventry City (on left) and JOHN ROBERTSON, Nottingham Forest, show the type of, "I'll-be-first" determination that's a must for top flight footballers.

THAT MI££ION POUND LABEL

MIDDLESBROUGH'S MIGHTY ATOM, STAN CUMMINS, SPEAKS HIS MIND

TWELVE months ago I received the biggest compliment of my young life . . . Though the man who paid it, Sheffield Wednesday manager, Jack Charlton, later admitted he hadn't meant it in quite the way it was picked up by the newspapers and television.

It seems Jack was talking about the transfer-market five or six years from now. He suggested it would be the time of the million pound deal.

He reckoned that kind of money would be changing hands for 'strikers' in the 25 to 26 age group. He used my name as an example of the sort of player he meant.

The headlines next day blazed out that my former Middlesbrough boss believed I'd be the very first

£1,000,000 player. Not quite true, of course. Jack had only hinted I might be one of those to fetch such a fee.

But, even allowing for that, I still feel flattered that Jack should value my ability so highly. Particularly as I seem to have been in the game only five minutes.

It was only midway through last season, that I started to get a regular game in the Middlesbrough first team. I'm still learning my soccer trade.

But, obviously, I do have ambitions . . . big ones. To be the best goalscorer in the country and help Boro win the game's major honours, will do for starters.

I hope, too, some day I will be considered good enough to play for England.

If, in the process, I become one of the first players to be involved in a £1,000,000 transfer I don't suppose I'll complain, either.

But, I find it hard to believe that much money will ever change hands for just one player. I wonder if anyone can ever be worth so much.

If it happened to me it would make me worth more than my weight or height in gold! £7,463 for every pound I weigh, or £15,763 for every single inch I stand off the ground. That's what it would mean.

At 5 ft. 3½ in. and 134 pounds, I'm one of the smallest blokes playing in full-time English football. Indeed, so far, that is probably my one real claim to fame.

I'm often asked if I find my size, or rather lack of it, a hindrance or a help.

It's a difficult question . . . simply because it isn't something I've ever paid a great deal of attention, to.

I've always believed if you have the talent and a little bit of luck, you can make it in football, whatever your size.

I know plenty of little 'uns who have been told that they would never make it in the big-time because of lack of inches. But that has never once happened to me.

Certainly, it didn't stop Middlesbrough signing me or giving me the big break in the First Division.

I like to think I've already proved that I'm physically equipped to take the knocks the game serves up.

From the experience I've gained in the game so far, I don't think I take any more 'stick' than the next bloke because of my size.

It may appear that way sometimes. A big fella coming in to tackle can look awkward because he towers over me. I often feel sorry for big defenders.

In some cases they've only to lift their boot a few inches off the ground and it looks as if they are scything me down at chest height. It can appear vicious . . . but seldom is.

It's because of this that I've always made a big effort to play the game fairly.

I simply don't believe in play-acting or feigning injury when bowled over in a tackle . . . even when it is a foul.

That kind of kidology can land a fellow professional in trouble with referees . . . and you with a reputation for being a 'cheat'.

The only 'reputation' I want is that of a good player who has made nothing but friends because of his sportsmanship out on the pitch.

Now that would mean more to me than any £1,000,000 transfer!

89

LOOKING FOR A GOAL?

Despite the glare of the sun, LOU MACARI, Manchester United, keeps a sharp eye on the action.

KENNY CLEMENTS, Manchester City

FORGOTTEN MAN WAS WEMBLEY MATCH-WINNER

MY first League game for Ipswich was against Arsenal in the opening match of last season. I scored and we won 1-0.

Just over eight months later Ipswich again beat Arsenal 1-0, and we took the F.A. Cup back to East Anglia.

I didn't score in the final. But I had a hand in the goal. Beating Sammy Nelson, the Arsenal full-back, I put across a centre. Willie Young pushed it into the path of Roger Osborne, who scored.

It was a fantastic occasion.

Two days before the game I was wondering whether I would even be in the side at Wembley. Two days afterwards I was picked for the England ' B ' team to tour New Zealand, Malaysia and Singapore.

In four days I had jumped from an unknown who who had played twenty-two games for Ipswich, plus a few as sub, to an England "B" team man.

During the season I had thought that as a 20-year-old I might have a chance of getting into an England Under-21 squad. Not so much as a first-teamer, but as a reserve sitting on the bench.

Instead I moved out of the Under-21's altogether and went off on a " B " trip with many senior England players.

All because of a wonderful occasion for Ipswich. We upset the odds and took the F.A. Cup to Portman Road for the first time.

Only one thing upset me. There was no mention of me in the programme.

My name was not included among the Ipswich players. But this was something that had been happening all season.

David Geddis kept creeping into the team. Every one seemed to be saying " who? "

It even happened after the final.

Mrs Margaret Thatcher, the leader of the Conservative party, watched the final.

Afterwards she was asked to name her No. 1 player.

" No. 10," she replied. " Trevor Whymark ."

No one had told her that there was a programme change. That No. 10 was David Geddis.

I started the season with Ipswich aware that I was a second choice striker—to Paul Mariner or Trevor Whymark.

I played in the final as a kind of mid-field right winger.

Everyone since has said it was the brilliant tactical move by Bobby Robson that beat the Arsenal.

To put Arsenal full-back, Sammy Nelson, under pressure. To prevent him starting attacks, and overlapping on the left hand side of the field.

It was a move that came as a surprise to many people—including me!

The match before we went to Wembley we played Aston Villa and lost 6-1.

After that defeat Bobby Robson, the Ipswich

DAVID GEDDIS — talks of the switch that brought Cup Final glory
Ipswich Town

92

THE FINAL CAPPED IT ALL

manager, called the players together. He said that everyone in the side must be prepared to switch around.

" That's apart from David Geddis." he explained. "He's just a centre-forward!"

On the Friday before we played the Arsenal we had our team talk and I was told to play wide on the right. To be anything else but an old fashioned centre-forward.

We won the F.A. Cup—and I went off with the England " B " side to the Near East and New Zealand.

Convinced that I can play anywhere—striker, containing right winger or central defender.

An important part of my career was the spell I had on loan with Luton Town.

I was on the fringe of the Ipswich side and I was offered the chance to move to Luton for a loan period. I expected to go straight into the Luton team. But they were going well and winning matches so I had to sit and wait for seven matches. Then I played nine games in the League side, with four as " sub ".

When I returned to Ipswich at the start of last season it gave me the experience to go straight into the Ipswich first-team squad. As cover for inter-nationalists like Paul Mariner and Trevor Whymark.

I'll always feel that the spell I had with Luton had a lot to do with earning me a place in the Ipswich Final side.

At Luton I got to know Eric Morecambe—the taller half of Morecambe and Wise.

On TV he tipped Ipswich to beat the Arsenal—because he knew David Geddis.

On final day I received a telegram.

" Congratulations—go out and win— Eric Morecambe."

Yet last season I had been very near to becoming a permanent Luton player. I even went on a close season tour with the club to New Zealand, Fiji and the United States.

When I came back I did not know whether I was to stay with Luton or rejoin Ipswich.

I went back to Ipswich, scored in the opening League game against the Arsenal and then the final capped it all.

I joined Ipswich as a sixteen-year-old from Carlisle, recommended by the same scout who had sent Kevin Beattie to Portman Road.

I knew Kevin Beattie. He was a little older than me, but we had both been at the same schools in Carlisle—St. Cuthbert's and Newman's.

Kevin Beattie helped me to fit in at Ipswich. There are not many players who have moved from Carlisle down south. It was nice to find a senior player already on the staff.

To me the worst part of playing at Wembley was the build-up.

I was injured and missed the semi-final against West Bromwich Albion.

After that match it was almost a month before the Wembley game.

It was a busy spell. Personal appearances, recording sessions, TV, newspaper men. There hardly seemed a spare minute.

On the Wednesday before the Wembley game we moved to a hotel in Hertfordshire. I felt drained from all the pre-final build-up. On reflection, it probably stopped us thinking too much about the game.

Everyone was fit. Trevor Whymark and Colin Viljoen had played. Both were internationalists. I began to wonder if I would be in the side.

Then manager Bobby Robson named his team and we had that Friday night team talk. Something of a change because the team talk was originally scheduled for Saturday morning.

" I want you to play wide on the right," said Mr Robson.

" Arsenal start so many attacks through left – back Sammy Nelson. Stay with him. Stop him getting the ball and attacking down the flanks. And get a goal as well!"

In the end it was Roger Osborne who got the goal. Ipswich proved the country club was more than a match for the team from the big city.

DAVID GEDDIS, Ipswich, hits the deck in a bid to hold Arsenal high-flyer, LIAM BRADY.

ROGER DAVIES,
Leicester City.

Joined Derby County from Southern League Worcester City in 1972, then moved on to Belgian club Bruges before returning to England on a £145,000 transfer to Filbert Street.

PAUL RANDALL.
Bristol Rovers.

One of the top goal scorers of last season. Bristol Rovers signed him from Rothman's Western league outfit, Frome Town.

ALAN TAYLOR,
West Ham.

Spotted by Rochdale while playing in the Northern Premier League with Morecambe. £45,000 took him to Upton Park and in his first season he bagged the two goals that won West Ham the FA Cup in the Wembley final against Fulham.

MICKY BURNS,
Newcastle.

Played for Skelmersdale in 1967 Amateur Cup final then moved to Blackpool. Transferred to Newcastle in 1974 for £180,000 plus.

NON-LEAGUE NURSERY

FRANK CARRODUS,
Aston Villa.

Product of Northern Premier League Altrincham. Manchester City picked up the midfield player on a small fee then sold him to Aston Villa for £100,000 in 1974.

*N*ON - LEAGUE teams have a reputation as cup giant-killers. Remember Blyth Spartans? But they've also proved a valuable nursery for the big league clubs, providing players like these who've made their mark in upper circles.

TREVOR LEE,
Millwall.

With team-mate Phil Walker, joined the Lions from Athenian League side Epsom and Ewell in 1976.

PETER SUDDABY,
Blackpool.

Another Skelmersdale product. An inspiring skipper, he has over 250 games for the Seasiders behind him.

GORDON HILL,
Derby County

Picked up by Millwall from Isthmian League side Southall, a club which also bred West Ham United's Alan Devonshire. Manchester United took Hill to Old Trafford before his £275,000 transfer to Derby County.

HOW NOW, WIMBLEDON?

A LOOK BACK AT THEIR FIRST-EVER SEASON IN THE FOOTBALL LEAGUE

IN the sporting world, the name Wimbledon used to stand for only one thing—tennis. Then Wimbledon Football Club arrived.

As a Southern League team they shook top outfits like Leeds United, Burnley and Middlesbrough in the FA Cup.

They won three successive Southern League titles, the Southern League Cup twice, two non-league Championship Challenge Cups and a London Senior Cup double.

Elected to the Football League last season and sandwiched between Chelsea and Fulham, with Queen's Park Rangers and Brentford not so far away, there were a lot of doubts about their ability to bridge the gap between non-league football and the Fourth Division.

But they've done well, finishing a respectable halfway in the table with their gates more than doubled. If they had started as they finished, the club would have been involved in the promotion battle.

Wimbledon started last season on a part-time set-up. When things did not go right they switched to full-time players. Signing established men like Ray Goddard (Millwall), and paying a club record £16,000 for Les Briley (Hereford).

In January they changed managers. Switching from Alan Batsford, the man behind their FA Cup and non-league success, to Dario Gradi, who had League experience as coach with Chelsea and Derby County.

They've developed the ground and the facilities in the Wimbledon area, building up a youth set-up that involves running four teams.

They own their own pub—the Sportsman—and have opened Nelson's—a night club and disco.

The club also has ambitious plans to turn Plough Lane into a sports and social centre for the Wimbledon area. They already have a modern weight-lifting gym open to all people in the area.

" At Wimbledon we hope to make everyone feel part of the club," says chairman Ron Noades.

It's a new approach to football in the London district.

DARIO GRADI — he took charge

The South-West London club has proved they can survive in an area dominated by Chelsea and Fulham.

" We have local people—and local youngsters—interested in the club," says manager Dario Gradi.

" A local youngster now walks into the club and asks for a trial. Until last season he would not have thought beyond Chelsea and Fulham."

Dave Smith, the manager who took Southend to promotion last season, feels that Wimbledon will be promotion contenders this term.

" Last season they were just not used to losing," he says. " In the Southern League they had been successful for too long. It took them time to adjust. They did it by the end of the season."

Now, like Dave Smith, many people are convinced the " Wimbledon Wombles " will make an impact in their new sphere.

The last London club to be elected to the Football League was Thames F.C. in 1930. They lasted two seasons. This is the second season for Wimbledon in the competition. They are determined it won't be THEIR last.

These young autograph hunters took their chance to capture BOB LATCHFORD, Everton and England, during a break in training.

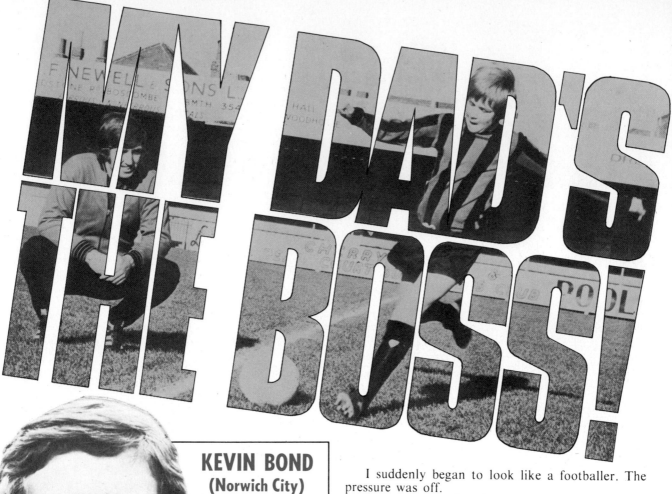

MY DAD'S THE BOSS!

**KEVIN BOND
(Norwich City)
on the
special
problems when
father and son
team up**

THERE'S only one football manager in the country who would have signed me as an apprentice.
He's my dad . . .

at 15 I was barely 5 ft. 5 in. tall, slow and not very strong.

But my father believed he could make me a professional footballer. He thought he could work on dispelling my faults and bringing out my assets. For I was a good passer and could read the game quite well.

Dad risked his reputation by signing me for Bournemouth when other managers probably would not.

I knew I had to justify my dad and make the grade. It meant working as hard as I possibly could not to let him down.

For two years I found the training very hard. I was shattered every day. My progress was slow.

Then in the space of a year I grew six inches and put on two stone in weight.

I suddenly began to look like a footballer. The pressure was off.

Last season I played over 25 first team matches for Norwich City. But I won't be satisfied until I can regard myself as a cast-iron first-team regular.

However, I believe that by playing in 21 successive First Division fixtures I have proved my father was right in giving me a start.

And his decision to take me from Bournemouth to Norwich after he had changed clubs was the right one, too.

Taking me on his staff was the only advantage I ever got from my dad.

He's always treated me the same as any other player.

I've had no favours in selection or in training. I get bawled out as much as any other clubmate.

Obviously it has been said I'm in the team only because my dad is the manager. I hope last

**JOHN BOND
— *no favours
from him***

98

BAD NEWS IN THE KITCHEN

season proved I'm worth my place on merit.

People have said it would be better for me to go to a different club. To get away from my dad just so no one could ever accuse him of favouritism.

But I have never felt the need to move. I don't know what it would be like anywhere else.

I know Tommy Docherty sent his son to Burnley because he felt it would be best all round for him to make his own way in the game.

But while at Stoke, Tony Waddington had his son, Steve, in the side when he was the manager there, and that didn't seem to cause any problems.

GOLDEN RULE

I've always had a very good relationship with my dad. He's never tried to push me into football as a career.

When I was young he would kick a ball around in the park with me. But he didn't give me any real coaching or say he wanted me to become a professional. He was always too busy playing, coaching or managing to come and watch me play.

He only started to help me after I joined Bournemouth, and even then I was treated just the same as the other juniors.

It's just coincidence that I'm a right-back like my dad. There's no question of trying to copy him.

It's a real disappointment to me that I was never old enough to appreciate his play when I did watch him. I don't remember much about his matches.

I can remember seeing the 1964 Cup Final at Wembley, when dad was in the West Ham team that beat Preston 3-2. But I was only six, and too young to know anything about the game.

After that he joined Torquay United for a couple of seasons. But I didn't watch him play, because we lived in London. Dad trained at West Ham, and travelled to Torquay for matches.

After Torquay he was coach to Gillingham, before taking over as manager at Bournemouth.

After matches nowadays, when we get home, dad will analyse my performance and go over the game.

He'll draw on his playing experience, but it's never a case of " I did this and that ". He's very fair.

There's one rule between us in discussing Norwich matches. We never talk about other Norwich players. The talk is kept to the team performance as a whole—and my game in particular.

When I first got into the side as a regular—for those 20 odd matches—I did well.

But I set myself a standard I found hard to maintain.

After a couple of not-so-good matches I could see what was coming.

It happened in the best possible way—another advantage of being the boss's son.

On a Thursday night my dad joined me in the kitchen at home and gave me the news.

He was leaving me out of the team. It wasn't a nice decision for him to make. It wasn't nice for me to hear. But at least I knew before the other players I was being left out.

Usually players would only know when the team was announced after training the day before the match.

I didn't get advance warning when I played my first full match against Aston Villa in 1977.

I was with the match squad in our hotel. Dad gave the pre-match talk and then announced the side—and I was in!

John Ryan, who was rested for that match, was the first man to wish me luck.

We lost 1-0, and I was left out of the next game, but I felt I'd done well.

A NERVOUS WAIT

Being told so near to the game gave me no time for the kind of nerves that hit me the first time I was picked for the first team—as substitute for a match against Leicester.

I came on for the last five minutes—and never touched the ball. All that worrying for nothing!

I know I have to work hard if I'm going to establish myself as a First Division regular. I need to be sharper—more lively.

If I am not the rest of my game can suffer. I must concentrate on developing this sharpness consistently.

But at least I feel now that with or without my dad as the manager, I can earn a living from football.

Some fans like to give me some stick because of my family connection, but I have the confidence to be able to ignore it.

The best part for me is that the other players at Norwich accept me as one of them.

Fortunately I get on very well with John Ryan, who moved into mid-field when I came into the team last season.

John said to me that if someone was to stay with the club for a week, watching the training and matches, without knowing players' names, at the end of it he wouldn't be able to pick out who was the manager's son.

I'm proud that I can be accepted like that. Proud too that my dad backed me in the first place.

I hope I will continue to justify his confidence.

● JOHN RYAN
— first to wish
me luck

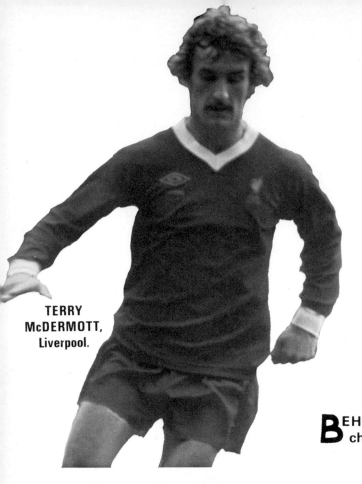

TERRY McDERMOTT, Liverpool.

RIGHT DRESS

BEHIND the scenes at Umbro. Just one of the firms churning out football strips in all sorts of colours —and for all kinds of clubs.

How it all begins—rolls of coloured cloth in the stockroom.

Cut down to size—rolls are trimmed to more manageable lengths

Taking shape—thick wads of cloth begin to look more like a football jersey.

The club emblem is stitched on—this time it's Liverpool's.

Nimble fingerwork is needed at this stage of sewing-up.

Where it all happens—a view of the factory.

Sorting out a pile of completed garments.

Inspection time—a sharp eye checks for flaws.

Ironing out any snags—a final press before the next stage.

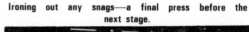

Packed and parcelled—ready to be sent out all over the country.

A sample of just some of the club jerseys that are made at this factory.

CRUNCH!!

*THE kind of action that thrills the fans! In a goalmouth clash, **TOMMY CUNNINGHAM** of Queen's Park Rangers is outnumbered by Newcastle defenders.*

ALL CHANGE AT STATION PARK

A moment's respite for the Forfar players before the extra-time against Rangers.

IN the biggest game in their 94-year-history, the 1977—78 Scottish League Cup semi-final, Second Division Forfar Athletic held mighty Glasgow Rangers to a draw over ninety minutes before being beaten in extra-time. Their share of the pooled " semi " gates was £4,600.

By all standards of the moment that was scant return in such a late stage of a major competition.

But it was also the biggest haul the wee Angus club has made from any game.

During last season, their best for ages, gates of 1000 at their Station Park were hailed with delight.

Because, in previous years, crowds of 300 or so were the usual.

How Forfar existed on such returns is simply that they are the most carefully-run of clubs—with supporters always ready to help out.

Evidence of their good house-keeping in days long gone are to be found in beginning-of-the century cash books stowed away at Station Park.

See how they did it from these extracts from ledgers dated 1913 and 1920—with the currency of that time turned into pence of today

ARCHIE KNOX, Forfar player-manager.

1913

TEAM v LOCHGELLY SEPT. 20th. 1913

	WAGES	FARES	TEAS			
SCOTT	37½					
SKENE	15					37½
TURNBULL	15	6½	5			15
DOIG	20	6½	5			26½
CHAPMAN	15	6½	5			31½
LEIGHTON	12½					26½
EASSON	12½					12½
WALKER	15	6½	5			12½
McLEAN						26½
LANGLANDS						
PETRIE	15					
TRAINER	15					15
						15
LOCHGELLY HALF GATE						
REFEREE					17	19½
POLICE					1	
REFRESHMENTS						37½
BONUS TO PLAYERS	12 at 25p					19
					3	·00
					23	94½

1920

TEAM v ARBROATH AM. JAN. 17th. 1920

	WAGES	FARES	TEAS	LOST TIME		
SCOTT	37½					37½
SOUTAR	37½					37½
MOIR	37½					37½
JOHNSTONE	75	25	12½	15		127½
AIMER	37½	25	12½			75
LOWSON	37½					37½
MILLAR	37½					37½
COSGROVE	37½	25	12½			75
BROWN	37½					37½
LANGLANDS	100					100
PETRIE	37½					37½
TRAINER	37½					37½
GROUNDSMAN	37½					37½
GIBB	37½					37½
REFEREE	110		40	2½		152½
ARBROATH AM. SHARE OF GATE						5·00
REFRESHMENTS 21½ COCOA 9½ TURNSTILE 62½						93½
S. SCOTT WORK ON PARK 62½ PAY ENVELOPES 5						67½
GOV. TAX ON GATE & STAND DRAWINGS						340
						19·06
JAN. 24th. GOV. TAX ON GATE & STAND DRAWINGS						2 23½
JAN. 31st. " " " " "						2 46

103

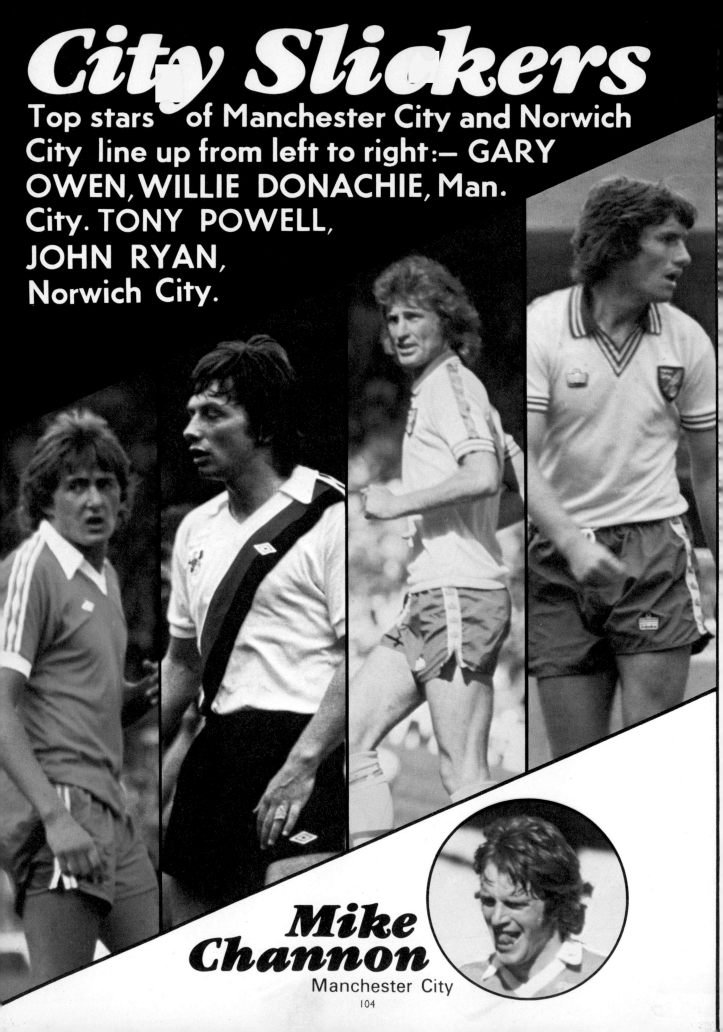

City Slickers

Top stars of Manchester City and Norwich City line up from left to right:— GARY OWEN, WILLIE DONACHIE, Man. City. TONY POWELL, JOHN RYAN, Norwich City.

Mike Channon
Manchester City

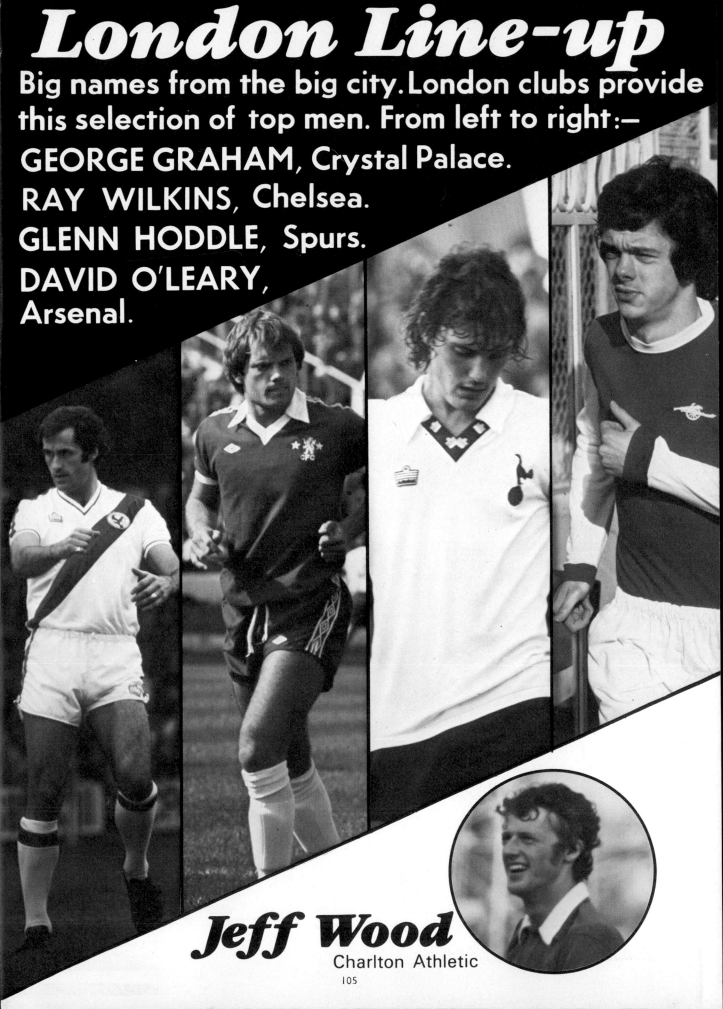

London Line-up

Big names from the big city. London clubs provide this selection of top men. From left to right:—

GEORGE GRAHAM, Crystal Palace.

RAY WILKINS, Chelsea.

GLENN HODDLE, Spurs.

DAVID O'LEARY, Arsenal.

Jeff Wood
Charlton Athletic

A HAMMER HITS

HOW DID YOU SCORE?

ANSWERS TO PUZZLES ON P.26

FAMOUS FACE

BECKENBAUER

LETTER LINKS

JORDAN, FRANCIS, LATCHFORD, WALLACE, CORRIGAN, CARR, TUEART, HAY.

106

WHOSE LEGS?

MALCOLM MACDONALD

HARD!

FOOTBALL CLUBS

1. HAMILTON ACADEMICALS
2. WEST BROMWICH ALBION
3. BOLTON WANDERERS
4. NOTTINGHAM FOREST
5. CREWE ALEXANDRA
6. DUNFERMLINE ATHLETIC

PYRAMID

A
1. FRY
2. BUSBY
3. BONETTI
4. GREENHOFF
5. NORTHAMPTON
6. CRYSTAL PALACE

CROSSWORD

¹R	²I	³M	M	³E	R		⁴F	⁵L	I	⁶G	H	⁷T
A		U		V		⁸C	U	R		O		R
⁹M	I	L	N	E		¹⁰L	E	T	D	O	W	N
S		L		¹¹R	A	Y		O		O		I
¹²E	V	E	N	T		¹³D	Y	N	¹⁴A	M	I	C
Y		R		O		E		I		S		S
	¹⁵L	Y	¹⁶O	N	S		¹⁷L	¹⁸I	M	¹⁹P	S
²⁰S			W				²¹B		P		R	²²C
²³C	H	²⁴E	L	²⁵S	E	A		²⁶S	T	E	E	L
O		V		K		²⁷G	O	W		S		A
²⁸R	E	A	D	I	N	G			²⁹I	N	T	E	R
E		N		L		Y			C		O	K
³⁰R	E	S	U	L	T		³¹C	H	A	N	C	E

CLUB FACTS

TOTTENHAM HOTSPUR

107

108   **TOMMY TAYLOR, West Ham United**

GARY PENDREY, Birmingham City

MY SISTER'S A BETTER PLAYER THAN ME....

JOKES ARSENAL ACE GRAHAM RIX

SOMETIMES I wake up in the morning and think, " Oh, no, not training again!"

Then, a few seconds later, I'm out of bed ready to get cracking. Because as soon as I start feeling depressed at having to train I have to admit how lucky I am to be playing football for a living.

I'm doing something I love—and getting paid for it.

I'm luckier than most footballers to be playing the game—at one stage I thought my career was over before it had really started!

"LUCKIER THAN MOST"

After a year as an apprentice with Arsenal I started to get pain in my back. The doctor thought it was simply a strained joint. So I carried on playing.

It turned out to be two cracked vertebrae, and I ended up in a plaster cast for twelve weeks. When it was taken off I was so weak I just flopped on the ground! I wondered if I'd ever have the strength to kick a ball again.

However, after about three weeks I was able to start training. Since then I've been clear of trouble—although I do still get the odd twinge. I still have to be careful.

For instance I'd give anything to be able to join the other lads in a game of golf. But I'm banned from swinging a club! It's thought the twisting movement might damage my back.

I'm also very light in the body. I get knocked off the ball easily.

Yet I'm a lot heavier than when I first arrived at Highbury. My first visit to the dressing room scales barely shifted the needle. It registered 8 stone 10 lbs. Now I'm up to over 10 stone—but I'm still looking for a few more pounds.

I just have to work hard on my game to get by on skill alone. Diets don't seem to work.

I must be one of the few players to have appeared in front of a 75,000 crowd at Wembley before making his league debut.

It was in the final of a special 6-a-side competition organised by a holiday camp firm. The final was played at Wembley before the 1976 Charity Shield match between Southampton and Liverpool.

I will always remember every detail, because it looked at one time if it would be my only big match.

Special rules gave 4 points for every goal, and one point for a corner. In the final with Leicester City we were 5 points to 0 ahead at half-time. But they came back and with 90 seconds to go were leading us 10-5.

One of our players, Ian McLeod, then scored the best goal I've ever seen anywhere. A great volley that gave the 'keeper no chance. With the last kick of the match, Steve Gatting—his brother Mike is a Middlesex and England cricketer—scored again to make it 13-10 to us.

We did a lap of honour. To us it was like winning the F.A. Cup.

A few days later X-rays showed my damaged back. I was put into plaster, at first for six weeks. When a specialist took a look he wasn't very happy, and put another ' corset ' on for a further six weeks.

That's when I started worrying about my career. Wishing I had studied harder at school and that kind of thing. I couldn't do anything. Couldn't even do up my own shoes. I was bored stiff.

I tried to solve that by buying a book on card playing. I learned how to play about 150 different games. That put me one or two up on the other lads at Highbury. Now, on away trips, I'm always the one with the pack of cards!

It was while I was in plaster I realised I had joined

"A DECISION I'VE NEVER REGRETTED"

the right club.

Arsenal sent me home to Yorkshire to be with my family. But when they had a match at Leeds they collected me from home, took me to the team hotel, and treated me just like one of the top squad—even though I was just a youth team player.

I went in the dressing room and was part of the set-up, and that was a tremendous boost for me. I realised I was more than just a face at Arsenal.

It had been a toss-up between Arsenal and Leeds United when I decided to turn senior. As a schoolboy I had been wanted by both.

ADVICE FROM ALAN BALL

As a kid I'd always been a Leeds fan. All I had ever wanted was to play for them. I kept saying that to my dad.

But when Leeds offered me a place as an apprentice I wasn't sure. They seemed to be buying a lot of players instead of bringing on the youngsters as in the past.

Then chief scout, Gordon Clark, took me to Highbury and showed me the Arsenal set-up. I was very impressed with the way young players were given a chance.

I decided on Arsenal—and have never regretted it.

Alan Ball was the big star when I first joined Arsenal. But he was never too big to help the youngsters. It means so much to a raw kid to be even spoken to by one of the top players. To be helped in any way is fantastic.

Alan Ball saw me play in a reserve match. Later he sorted me out. " You're clever, but you are one-

WILLIE YOUNG —lone Scot

paced," he told me. " You must sharpen up to make the most of what you've got."

I felt ten feet tall. Next day I was working on my sprinting.

Alan Ball has always had a great temperament for football. He never knows when he is beaten. I like

to think I have the same approach. I'm a rotten loser. I hate losing at anything—including cards.

My brother Ian is probably a better player than I am. But he doesn't really care about football. He's not bothered whether he wins or loses. Just plays for fun. He wants a career outside football.

Actually the best footballer in the family is neither myself nor my brother. It's my sister Lisa!

No kidding! She's got better control of the ball than me. Lisa can keep the ball up in the air for ages, with several hundred touches. I've got no chance against her—and she is only 16.

The skill I have was developed at home. I used to play back alley " squash " with a football.

Between my home and next door, in the village of Campsall, near Doncaster, is an alley. I'd spend hours kicking a football against the walls, volleying the rebounds, learning the angles. Just like squash played with the feet. It developed my control and ability to strike the ball well.

My strength is in passing the ball. I'm not a great dribbler like Liam Brady. I like to knock the ball off short or long. That's why I play better in away games. In our set-up I play deeper in mid-field away from home. So I get the chance to use the ball.

The matches at Highbury I have to play further up, as a kind of left-winger. I feel a bit restricted there.

I know I still have to work on all aspects of my game—in particular my right foot. I'm trying to become as good with the right as with my more natural left.

HANGMAN'S NOOSE

I'm not a bad header of the ball. That's due to my hangman's noose. Back home my dad rigged up a ball hanging on the end of a rope for me to practise jumping.

The spirit at Highbury is very high, with all sorts of ' mickey-taking ' on the side. Big-hearted Willie Young usually has to put up with much of it. That's because he is something of an odd-man-out at Highbury.

In the first team squad are four or five Englishmen, three Northern Ireland and three Eire internationalists. Willie Young is the lone Scot.

On Saturdays the team usually watch the lunchtime football preview programmes on television. There's usually an item on Scottish football. When it comes on Liam Brady will start the kidology by singing " Flower of Scotland ".

Willie sometimes rises to the bait, but he's good natured enough to know we are just " having him on ". The big fellow is a popular team member, though it must be hard going for him when there are at least six Irishmen spreading the blarney round the room.

Last season ended in a big disappointment for all of us at Highbury—losing to Ipswich in the Cup final.

It was a great experience for me, even if I only played for part of the game as substitute. I'm sure we we can go one better this season and win one of the major trophies.

The Dalglish Diary

How It All Happened For Kenny — The New King of the Kop.

MILESTONES OF A HECTIC ELEVEN MONTHS

AUGUST 11, 1977

Kenny Dalglish leaves Glasgow Celtic to join English and European Champions Liverpool for £440,000. A record fee for a deal involving two British clubs.

Anfield boss Bob Paisley sees Dalglish as the replacement for Kevin Keegan, transferred to SV Hamburg for £500,000.

Says Paisley, " By signing Kenny we have got one of the best, if not the best, players in Britain. I bought him because he has so much ability.

" I want the same thirst for success at Liverpool we have always had. This signing shows we are not letting the grass grow under our feet."

And Kenny says, " I'm told Kevin Keegan wanted a new challenge. That's what I want. With Celtic I got into the habit of collecting silverware. It's one I want to continue."

AUGUST 13

Dalglish makes an impressive debut in Liverpool colours in the Charity Shield. A Wembley repeat of last season's FA Cup final against Manchester United. It ends in a 0-0 draw.

Paisley enthuses, " I was pleased with Kenny's performance. He reads the game well.

" He's a very unselfish player. He'll cause other teams a lot of problems."

Dalglish says of his welcome: " The supporters have made me feel at home. I don't expect any difficulty settling in."

AUGUST 20

League debut time. Kenny makes the headlines with his first-ever goal for the Merseyside club.

It takes only seven minutes of the away match at Middlesbrough for the new boy to get himself on the scoresheet. He tucks away Terry McDermott's through ball for Liverpool's goal in a 1—1 draw.

AUGUST 30

Another debut goal! This time in the League Cup. Kenny sets the ball rolling on Liverpool's march to Wembley with his side's first against Chelsea at Anfield.

SEPTEMBER 17

Kenny scores in a 1—1 draw at Ipswich. His sixth in seven games for 'Pool. Already Kevin Keegan's name is being rapidly pushed to the back of the fans' minds. Anfield hails the new KING OF THE KOP.

SEPTEMBER 21

Back on Scotland duty for the vital World Cup qualifier with Czechoslovakia at Hampden Park. The Liverpool man heads the third goal which clinches a 3—1 victory for the Scots.

It's a goal which sets-up a World Cup decider —Wales v Scotland at Anfield.

" It gives me a great kick that the game will be at Anfield," says Kenny. " I already consider it my home though I've been here just a few weeks."

OCTOBER 12

Wales v Scotland at Anfield. The match is played in Liverpool as no ground in Wales was considered capable of holding the vast crowd expected.

In front of the Kop, Kenny heads in Martin Buchan's cross to clinch a 2-0 victory and a place in the World Cup finals for his country. It is Dalglish's 50th game for Scotland.

The day it all began. Kenny Dalglish signs for Liverpool, watched by Liverpool chairman, John Smith (left), manager Bob Paisley (centre) and club secretary Peter Robinson.

A VITAL GOAL FOR LIVERPOOL

JANUARY 7, 1978

Kenny keeps up his run of debut goals in domestic competitions for Liverpool. It's against Chelsea in the Third Round of the FA Cup.

However, it's not enough to stop the Merseysiders being beaten.

JANUARY 17

Glory night for Kenny at Wrexham! He hits his first ever hat-trick for Liverpool in a 3—1 win over the Welsh giant-killers in the League Cup.

"Terry McDermott put two on a plate for me," he concedes. "But every goal gives you pleasure no matter how it comes."

FEBRUARY 7

Dalglish among the goals. He hits Liverpool's first in a 2—1 win over Arsenal in the first leg of the League Cup semi-final.

A goalless draw in the return at Highbury is enough to send Kenny back to Wembley for the second time this season.

MARCH 28

Dalglish the goal-maker. He provides the cross for David Johnson to score against Borussia Munchengladbach in the away leg of the European Cup semi-final.

APRIL 12

The second leg of the European Cup semi-final against Borussia Munchengladbach. Liverpool make their way to a 3—0 victory—and Kenny grabs one of the goals.

MAY 1

Dalglish keeps finding the net. A hat-trick against Manchester City bringing his season's total to 28.

MAY 11

Perhaps the most vital goal Liverpool have scored all season—and Kenny Dalglish gets it. It's the only goal in the Liverpool v Bruges European Cup Final—and Liverpool win the trophy for the second time in succession.

To cap a great week for Dalglish, he's named for Scotland's pool of players for the Home International Championship and the World Cup.

JUNE 7

It's a bad night for Scotland in the World Cup. They manage only a 1-1 draw with Iran after being beaten 3-1 by Peru. But it's another milestone for Dalglish. It's his 56th appearance for Scotland beating the previous total of 55 by Denis Law.

JUNE 11

Scotland end on a happier note by beating Holland 3—2. Kenny Dalglish notches the first of the three Scottish goals. Goodbye, Argentina . . .

Plenty to smile about. Kenny Dalglish with the European Cup after Liverpool's triumph.

On target for Scotland. Kenny Dalglish scores against Wales in their World Cup qualifying match.

THE WINDMILL MEN

THE CAMERA "FREEZES"— AND CATCHES THESE REMARKABLE MOMENTS OF FOOTBALL ACTION.

Flying high is STUART BOAM, Middlesbrough, in a bid to block a shot by Everton's MARTIN DOBSON.

ANDY LYNCH, Celtic, swoops in front of ANDY ROLLAND, ex-Dundee United now in America.

Poised as if for flight are DONATO NARDIELLO, Coventry, and MIKE PEJIC, Everton.

JACKIE CHARLTON

Tough Guy...

with a heart of gold

WITH Leeds United and England, Jack Charlton earned a reputation as a tough-tackling, give-nothing-away defender.

Then Jack moved on to the managerial side. First with Middlesbrough, then with Sheffield Wednesday. His no-nonsense approach added to his reputation. But there's another side to Jack Charlton. The warm, human touches that have earned him the regard of players and fans alike.

The other side of Jack Charlton is most obvious when dealing with youngsters. They often write to the Wednesday boss. Despite his heavy, football manager's schedule, Jack still finds time to send a signed reply to each one.

Lots of laddies send in requests to visit Hillsborough on match day. Whenever possible, it's the boss himself who acts as guide—some kids even wangle a seat in the trainer's dug-out!

Jack's touch with the youngsters also comes across in his coaching sessions for Television.

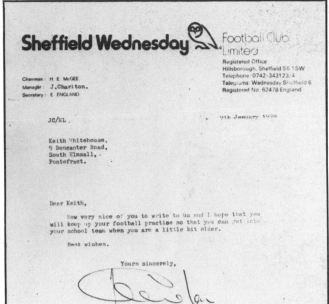

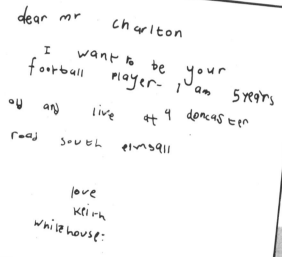

The Wednesday boss has also made his mark with the fans. Jack used to be a heavy smoker at Wednesday's matches. Noting that he was often fumbling in his pockets for matches a group of fans clubbed together to buy a cigarette lighter for him!

With his players, too, Jack shows those touches that can be so important in a happy club.

Last season he took a Wednesday squad to his parents' North Yorkshire farmhouse. A break from the routine of training.

The Charltons made all the players feel at home—and the visit' was voted a great success.

Just another example of the other side of tough guy Jack Charlton.

All smiles at breakfast! With Mrs Cissy Charlton, the players showing their faces are, from left to right— Richard Walden, Ken Knighton (coach, now Sunderland), Jimmy Mullen, Dennis Leman, Tommy Tynan, Dave Cusack.

QUEEN'S PARK –

THE ONE AND ONLY.

JOE GILROY, coach to the only amateur team in senior football, talks about his job.

OTHER clubs can only offer a player money— we can offer him his freedom. That to me is the reason for Queen's Park's continued presence in a game where money is so important.

As the only amateur club amongst the 130 in the Scottish and English leagues, we've obviously got our work cut out to attract quality players willing to play for enjoyment rather than gain.

But there are still a lot of youngsters keen to play football for exactly these reasons. In my first 18 months as coach at Hampden we gave trials to 140 boys. Every one eager to sign for our club.

Not all of these lads were accepted by us. Though, as we run four sides we normally carry a pool of just under 70 players. This gives you some indication of how big Queen's Park still is.

Looking after all these players takes a lot of organisation plus a lot of effort from every member of our splendid backroom staff.

It's noticeable that almost everyone connected with the running of the club is an ex-player. Once you've been connected with Hampden and tasted the atmosphere, you're hooked for life.

Once a Queen's Parker, always a Queen's Parker.

Past players like famous internationalist Jack Harkness of Wembley Wizard fame, Bobby Brown and Ian McColl who both played for and managed Scotland, and Bobby Clark who was in Argentina as a member of our World Cup squad, are always getting in touch with us recommending youngsters they feel would make good players for our club.

It's important that this continues because our future depends on getting these young boys.

The average ages of my first team, second team, and third team are all under 20! I'd go as far as to say we've probably got the highest number of quality youngsters in the country. There are lots of professional clubs who would give a lot for some of our young players.

Some people keep asking if there is still a place for an amateur side in today's game.

Well, my answer to that is a clear YES, as many of today's top players will tell you.

We don't just take youngsters straight from school and squeeze every ounce of talent we can get out of them before throwing them on the scrapheap.

I like to ask rather than tell people to do things at Hampden. No-one is ordered to attend training, for example. The players come because they want to.

But I'm not kidding myself. I realise most of their football in the future is likely to be spent elsewhere. If we can sign the right players, bring them up through the reserve sides and give them a chance in the first team to show what they can do, then the best are going to be the targets of the big professional sides.

Every year at the end of April, all our players become free agents as we only register them for a year at a time. If they decide to accept an offer from a professional club, then they go with our good wishes. They are not held at Hampden by pieces of paper, only by choice.

And so, inevitably, I must look upon my task as never-ending. Every time I get some useful players in my side, I'm liable to lose them and see my side broken up.

But that's why we've got so many lads on our books to maintain the standard when we lose our best lads.

Some day soon I hope I can keep a good side together long enough to enable us to climb out of the Second Division, and perhaps even reach the Premier League. That's my aim and that of all at Hampden.

Then we would show everyone that even if Queen's Park are amateur by name, they're very professional in approach.

IT HAPPENED

1 – Two players scored four goals on their debuts for new clubs after being transferred. Names?

2 – A player became the second youngest manager ever — then resigned ten months after his appointment. Who?

3 – A Scottish team scored most league goals in Britain. Which team?

4 – He scored a hat-trick on his debut for the England Under-21 side — and never played again for them last season. His name was?

5 – Three managers took their sides to promotion from the Third Division after their first season in the hot seat. Name them and their clubs.

6 – Scotland's "Manager of the Year" had had only one full season as team boss. Who was he?

7 – He was sent off two minutes after coming on as substitute in the first game of the season. Who was he?

20 TESTING

8 – Which player scored England's first goal under Ron Greenwood?

9 – His team were knocked out in the F.A. Cup second round, yet this manager still reached semi-final. Who was he?

10 – Which two teams lost out on promotion through goal difference?

It's Liverpool goalkeeper Ray Clemence with a desperate race on his hands to beat that ball to the goal. Ray had the last laugh—the ball went past the post.

LAST SEASON • •

11 – A Scottish team celebrated their centenary by winning promotion. Name?

12 – **Name the player who won a League Cup winners' tankard with Nottingham Forest, yet never played a League game all season.**

QUESTIONS

13 – Which team won the Anglo-Scottish Cup?

14 – **With his last kick of the game he scored last season's F.A. Cup Final winner. Who was he?**

15 – Which game was seen at two different grounds at the same time?

16 – **Six players from the same club played for England against Switzerland. The club and players?**

17 – A Scottish Second Division team won more games away than at home. Which one?

18 – **Only two sides were unbeaten in the League on their home grounds. Can you name the two?**

19 – Two players who finished with promotion medals each started the season with eventually relegated First Division sides. Name the players, their new club, and from whence they were transferred.

20 – **Who scored a hat-trick of penalties in a game and still ended up on the losing side?**

(Answers on page 125)

FULL HOUSE!

The crowded Partick Thistle goalmouth tells its own story of fierce pressure by the Rangers. And its pressure that paid off—with a final goal in a 3-3 thriller.

THE locals reckoned Slagton United the strongest team in the Football League. They were holding all the others up.

Struggling at the foot of the Fourth Division, United had to win their away game with Ramsley Athletic, or apply for re-election once more.

And this year they might not get enough votes.

On the morning of the game, a not very happy party gathered outside the United ground to catch their bus to Ramsley.

With Sandy Tyler, the player-manager, there were thirteen players, the entire playing strength, With them was Mr Walter Frost, the chairman of the club, who was also the trainer.

Jeff Adams, the striker, sat down on the hamper.

"Where's the bus, Sandy?" he asked. "Rollright coaches are always on time."

"We're not using them any more," said Sandy Tyler. "I got a cheaper price from another firm, Highway Express. They should be here by now. I'll take a look round."

As Sandy walked to the end of the wall enclosing the ground, a burly, red-faced young fellow came hurrying round the corner and bumped into Sandy.

"Oops!" said the young fellow. "Sorry, mate! Hello, you're Sandy Tyler. I was wondering where you'd got to. I'm Barney Bassett, your bus driver. I was just coming to look for you."

Sandy looked down the side street and saw a bus parked there.

"What are you doing in the side street?" he asked. "I told your firm to pick us up outside Door C."

Barney pulled a crumpled scrap of paper out of his pocket and peered at it.

"Door C, eh?" he said. "I thought it was Door G. The boss's handwriting ain't too good. Hang on, I'll bring the bus round."

He dashed back to the bus and Sandy winced as he heard the crashing of gears. The bus lurched forward, exhaust smoke gushing out. It bounced over the pavement as it turned the corner, and the waiting players stared at it.

The bus was small, with dents and scratches here and there. There were muddy streaks all over it, as if somebody had made a not very

THE LUCK OF BARNEY'S BUST-UP BUS

Take the road with Slagton United on a never to-be-forgotten day.

successful attempt to clean away several months' dirt.

"Blimey!" said Jeff Adams. "No wonder you got a lower price, Sandy! Is this what they call a Highway Express?"

Barney shoved the sliding doors open and jumped out, beaming.

"All aboard, gents!" he boomed.

"Er — are you sure you're a fully qualified bus driver?" said Sandy.

"You bet!" said Barney. "Mind you, I don't mind admitting I ain't in the James Hunt class. I've got this job because I come cheap! Actually, I'm a footballer! I'm on your books! Well, I had a trial with the United before you took over, Sandy. They said they'd let me know, but I've heard no more."

"We can't afford any new players just now, Barney," said Sandy. "Well, let's go. Give me a hand to load the kit."

Barney wrestled with a key in the lock of the boot at the back of the bus. He gave the panel a kick and the boot lid fell open.

"A bit temperamental, this bus," he said. "It's all right if you know how to handle it."

Barney and Sandy lifted the basket into the boot, then the players started to climb aboard. Jeff Adams was first. He was on the step when the door started to slide shut. As Jeff jumped back, the door jerked across and he fell, his leg trapped in the door.

His yell brought Sandy and Barney running. Barney hammered his fists on the door and it opened! Sandy and Mr Frost helped Jeff up.

"The door's a bit dodgy, too," said Barney.

"I can see that!" howled Sandy. "Get Jeff aboard, Mr Frost. Let's see what the damage is."

Barney followed the players aboard as Jeff slumped down into a seat.

"My ankle got a nasty wrench," he said. "I don't reckon I can play." He put his hand on the seat. "Hey, these seats are damp!"

"Er—yes," said Barney. "I tried to give the bus a bit of a clean up, see? I turned the hose on it, but there were a few leaks here and there. Still, the weather forecast says it ain't going to rain. We'll be on our way."

He settled himself at the wheel and the players bounced in their damp seats as the bus jerked forward.

After more crashes as Barney changed gear to take a steep hill, Pete Rogers, sitting in the back seat, heard a bang and a thump behind him, He looked out of the rear window. The boot lid had dropped open and the team's hamper had fallen out, and was skidding into the gutter.

"Hey, stop!" yelled Pete, jumping out into the aisle.

Barney stamped on the brakes. There was nothing wrong with them anyway. The bus stopped as if it had hit a wall, sending Pete flying forward to land face-down in the passage.

"My wrist!" yelped Pete. "I fell on it! I think it's broken!"

"Cor! Sorry, mate!" said Barney. "When you yelled, I thought there

was something desperately wrong."

"There is, you clown!" Pete shouted. "Our team's kit has fallen out!"

Barney and one of the players went back for the hamper. They stowed it away and slammed the boot lid shut.

Meanwhile, Walter Frost had been examining Pete's wrist.

"I'm afraid it's broken, Pete," he said. "We'll have to get you to hospital."

"There's one on the route," said Barney. "Here we go!"

At the hospital, Sandy and Mr Frost helped Jeff and Pete into the casualty department and left them in the care of the nurses.

"Only eleven men left!" said Sandy as he and Mr Frost came out. "No subs, no nothing! This journey's turning into a nightmare. We——"

His voice died away in a horrified screech. Barney and Mike Morton, the big centre-back, were carrying Derek Potter into the hospital.

"What — what's happened?" croaked Sandy.

"My bus seat gave way under me," said Mike. "Came down on Derek's foot with all my weight on it!"

"My foot's crushed flat!" howled Derek.

"Not quite as bad as that," said the doctor who examined him. "But you've got a cracked bone in the foot. No match for you today, my lad."

Sandy clutched at what hair he had left.

"Ten men!" he groaned. "I've

got to field a team with only ten men!"

"You've got me," said Barney. "What?"

"I'm on the United books as an amateur," said Barney. "It's in order for you to play me. I've got my boots in the bus. Always carry 'em in case I get the chance of a game somewhere."

"Well, at least he'd make up the numbers, Sandy," said Mr Frost. "What choice have we got?"

"My usual position is striker, but I'll play anywhere you like," said Barney.

"Cor!" said Sandy. "Come on, then!"

A SHOCK GOAL

AN hour later Barney swung the bus into the car park outside the Ramsley Athletic ground.

"How's that?" he said. "No more trouble! All present and correct!"

"We're not out of the bus yet!" said Sandy.

He held his breath. Barney was heading the bus for a narrow gap between the two parked cars. The bus slid in neatly and stopped.

"Spot on!" said Barney. "I'm pretty good at parking. Got an eye for it."

"That's where this bus should stay," said Sandy. "Permanently parked! Come on!"

Barney's beam stretched from ear to ear as he trotted out with the

team. He was wearing Jeff's No. 9 shirt and it fitted him like a second skin.

From the kick-off, Ramsley bustled into the attack. Hunting promotion, and favourites to win, they were a big, tough team.

Barney drifted back in midfield, watching the Ramsley winger running the ball along the line on the left.

As the winger crossed the ball, Barney positioned himself for a header. The Ramsley striker came crashing into him, climbed up his back and headed the ball on.

"Ugh!" said Barney, going down on his face.

He pushed himself up in time to see the United 'keeper scrambling a shot round the post. Barney moved into the goalmouth for the corner, but, as the ball came over, he was jerked back as a Ramsley man grabbed a handful of his shirt.

"Cor!" said Barney.

The ball dropped among a ruck of players and bounced about among lunging boots.

"I've had enough of being messed about!" grunted Barney.

He plunged forward. His shirt ripped up the back, leaving a piece in the hand of the player who was holding him. Players bounced to left and right as Barney ploughed through the ruck, and came away with the ball at his feet.

Barney kept running. He sprinted out of the penalty area and hared on. Sandy went after him.

"Move it, Barney!" he yelled.

A defender pounded in at Barney, eyes on the ball and Barney's feet, waiting for the swerve. Barney just went on in a straight line. The defender cannoned off him and sat down.

Barney took a quick look round. Now he was out on his own. Most of the players had moved up for the corner. Only one more defender and the Ramsley goalkeeper were in front of him.

The defender came sliding in. He wasn't bothered about the ball. He was going to get the man. But when Barney put on a spurt, the defender missed him and went slithering past.

Barney did a quick shuffle, and hit the ball on the run. The goalkeeper was still diving as the ball slammed into the net.

For a moment, the United team stood gaping. Any goal scored by the United came as a surprise, and

"WE DON'T WANT POLISH, WE WANT GOALS!"

Barney's goal was more surprising than most.

The grinning United men surrounded Barney, slapping him on the back.

"Why didn't the last manager use you?" demanded Sandy.

"He said I lacked polish," said Barney.

"And he was dead right!" grinned Sandy. "But we don't want polish, we want goals! Get stuck in, Barney!"

*   *   *   *

That goal had shaken Ramsley. They fell back as the United came at them again. Suddenly the United could see themselves actually winning an away game, and climbing away from the bottom of the table.

Barney had put on a spare shirt, but nobody tried to grab it again. Not that he was left alone. Two defenders went with him everywhere. Barney had got the opposition worried.

Sandy ran the ball towards the corner flag and lifted it over. Barney was by the near post, with defenders crowded round him. The goalkeeper moved across to cover the area by the post.

Barney had his back to the goal as the ball bounced in front of him. He turned slightly and let the ball slide off his foot.

"Hey, where did it go?" exclaimed one of the defenders.

A roar went up from the crowd. Sandy came prancing across.

"It's in the goal, mate!" said Barney.

The defenders looked round. Barney had glided the ball past them and the goalkeeper, into the net.

"What a fluke!" said one of the defenders.

"That was no fluke!" said Sandy. "But I don't know how you did it, Barney."

"It's like parking, see," said

Barney. "Told you I've got an eye for it. Just size up the gap and straight in!"

One goal had shaken Ramsley. A second from the lowly United was an insult that stung them into action. For a time they pinned the United back in their own half.

Barney had fallen back to help the defence. He got in the way of a shot from the Ramsley striker, and the ball bounced off him for a corner.

The rain bucketed down as the players moved up for the kick. When the ball came over wide of the goal, Barney and the Ramsley

striker ran for it. The Ramsley man slipped in the wet grass, and Barney swerved past him, pouncing on the ball.

"Barney's got good road-holding!" grinned Sandy, striding away.

Barney lifted the ball across to Sandy, and raced away down the middle through the mud. A defender came at Sandy and he tapped the ball to his inside man. The crowd yelled as the return pass found Sandy.

"Hey, that weather forecast was wrong!" said Barney. "It's starting to rain."

Barney splashed into the penalty area. Muddy puddles were growing near goal. Sandy swerved inside and lifted the ball across to Barney.

A defender strode in behind Barney. The ball dropped five

yards outside the goal and stopped dead in the mud. The goalkeeper started out as Barney raced towards the ball.

It looked like the goalkeeper's ball all the way, till Barney lunged forward, skidding through the mud. and with the toe of his boot cued the ball between the goalkeeper's legs and into the net.

Barney got to his feet, covered in mud, as the United players clamoured round him.

"Another of your bus-driving tricks, Barney!" chortled Sandy. "A controlled skid!"

When the referee blew for full-time, the jubilant United players escorted Barney off.

"A hat-trick!" said Sandy. "I'm signing you on here and now, Barney! Your bus-driving days are over!"

"Great!" said Barney. "But I've still got to drive you fellows home."

"Oh!" groaned Sandy, "I'd forgotten that!"

It was still raining when Barney drove the bus away from Ramsley. The players didn't have to look out of the windows to discover that the rain was sprinkling on them through holes in the roof. But an extra shower after the game could not dampen their spirits. They made the windows rattle with several choruses of "Singing in the Rain."

Halfway home, when darkness had come down, the bus stuttered to a halt on a deserted stretch of road. Barney got a torch and poked about under the bonnet.

"It may take some time to fix, boys," he said.

"Who cares?" said Sandy.

An A.A. patrolman finally came to the rescue of the stranded players and got the bus started.

"Beats me," the patrolman reported later. "Here were these fellows, stranded in the rain, miles from home. They were all falling about laughing and saying something about that beat-up old bus being their lucky mascot!"

• YOUR PICTURE GUIDE •

QUIZ ANSWERS — From pages 120-121

1—Joe Royle (Bristol City); Colin Lee (Tottenham Hotspur).
2—Alan Thompson (Stockport County).
3—Dundee—91 goals.
4—Peter Ward (Brighton).
5—Arfon Griffiths (Wrexham); John Docherty (Cambridge U.); Nobby Stiles (Preston).
6—Billy McNeill (Aberdeen) now Celtic manager.
7—Paul Hooks (Notts County).
8—Ray Kennedy (against Luxembourg).

9—Ron Atkinson. Cambridge were knocked out. Then Atkinson became boss of West Bromwich Albion.
10—Brighton (Second Division) and Peterborough United. (Third Division).
11—Clyde.
12—Chris Woods.
13—Bristol City.
14—Roger Osborne, Ipswich.
15—The UEFA Cup game between Manchester United and St Etinne was played at Plymouth's Home Park and

also shown on close circuit television at Old Trafford.
16—Liverpool. Ray Clemence, Phil Neal, Emlyn Hughes, Ray Kennedy, Terry McDermott and Ian Callaghan.
17—Meadowbank Thistle.
18—Nottingham Forest and Aldershot.
19—Frank Worthington and Alan Gowling left Leicester City and Newcastle Utd. respectively to join Bolton Wanderers.
20—Alan Slough (Peterborough United). (They were beaten 4-3 by Chester.)

Printed and published by D. C. Thomson & Co. Ltd., 185 Fleet Street, London EC4A 2HS.
© D. C. Thomson & Co. Ltd., 1978.